Ethics: Theory and Practice

Copyrighted Material

Ethics: Theory and Practice

Gotham City Ventures, LLC
500 Westover Dr. #6479
Sanford, NC 27330

http://www.gothamcityventures.com/

ISBN: 978-0-9964591-1-2
Copyright ©2015 by Gotham City Publishing
All rights reserved. None of the material found in this study guide may be reproduced without permission from the publisher.
Printed in the USA

Disclaimer/Liability Release:
The publication of this book is for the purpose of examination preparation. Gotham City Ventures does not guarantee the accuracy and completeness of the information contained herein and cannot claim liability in relation to the information or opinions contained within this study guide. Gotham city ventures will not be held liable for damages of any kind related to the materials found in this study guide.

Ethics: Theory and Practice

Steps to Achieving Success!

Step 1- Test Taking/Study Skills Review
Gain knowledge in test taking and study skills with over 25 pages of review! Increase your chances of passing the exam by determining your learning style, how to study well and strategies for approaching exam questions.

Step 2- Complete Content Review
Focus on the exam content with a comprehensive review. CreditPREP provides you with a well written and organized presentation of content within this manual and access to online, mobile friendly flashcards. These flashcards allow you to take advantage of every spare moment in your hectic life! Please utilize this valuable resource with the instructions below:

FLASHCARD ACCESS:

Please go to www.gothamcitypublishing.com
Click on CreditPREP Flashcards Registration
Follow the Directions Provided to Access the Flashcards

Step 3- Test Your Knowledge
Use the full length practice exam provided at the end of this manual to determine your knowledge of Developmental Psychology. Use the results of this exam to efficiently focus your final studying efforts.

Step 4- Take Your Exam
Apply the credits earned toward your college degree and future career!!

Ethics: Theory and Practice

Table of Contents

Table of Contents 3
Preparing for Your Ethics Exam 7
Study Skills 7
Scheduling Your Test 15
    Last Minute Preparation for Testing 15
Test-Taking Tips 16
    Multiple Choice Questions 18
    True / False Questions 19
    Matching Questions 20
    Essay Questions 21
Overcoming Test Anxiety 21
Introduction to your text: 25
General Course Objectives: 25
Chapter 1: Ethics and Ethical Reasoning 26
    Learning Objectives 26
    What is Morality? 26
    What is Ethics? 26
    Normative Ethics 26
    Non-Normative Ethics 28
    Moral Judgments, Argumentation, and Reasoning 28
    Argumentation: Basic Terms and Concepts 29
Chapter 1 Review Questions 31
Chapter 2: Ethical Relativism and Meta-ethics 33
    Learning Objectives 33
    Ethical Relativism 33
    Support for Ethical Relativism 34
    Criticisms of Relativism 34
    Other Meta-ethical Theories 35
Chapter 2 Review Questions 37
Chapter 3: Egoism, Contractarianism, and Utilitarianism 39
    Learning Objectives 39
    Egoism 39
    Contractarianism 40

- Utilitarianism 41
  - The Utilitarian Theorists 41
    - Utilitarian Justification 42
  - Subtypes of Utilitarianism 43
- **Chapter 3 Review Questions**..45
- **Chapter 4: Deontological Theories** 46
  - Learning Objectives 46
  - Deontological Ethics 46
  - Immanuel Kant..46
    - Second Formulation – The Formula of Humanity 48
  - The Formula of Autonomy 49
  - The Formula of the Kingdom of Ends 49
  - John Rawls 50
  - William David Ross 51
- **Chapter 4 Review Questions**..53
- **Chapter 5: Virtue Ethics, Natural Law Theory, Communitarianism, and Feminine Ethics** 54
  - Learning Objectives 54
  - Virtue Ethics 54
    - Soul 55
    - Virtue 55
    - The Mean 56
    - Morals 56
    - Eudemonia 56
  - Natural Law 57
    - Criticisms of Natural Law Theory 59
  - Communitarianism...59
    - David Hume 60
  - Feminine Ethics 62
- **Chapter 5 Review Questions**..64
- **Chapter 6: Existentialism and Nietzsche** 65
  - Learning Objectives 65
  - Existentialism...65
  - Nietzsche: On the Genealogy of Morals 65
  - Simone de Beauvoir 68

Ethics: Theory and Practice

- Chapter 6 Review Questions 70
- Chapter 7: Justice, Rights, and Liberty 71
  - Learning Objectives 71
  - Justice 71
  - Types of Justice 71
  - Rights 73
  - Liberty 74
  - Autonomy 75
  - Informed Consent 76
- Chapter 7 Review Questions 77
- Chapter 8: Abortion and Euthanasia 78
  - Learning Objectives 78
  - Abortion 78
  - Euthanasia 80
- Chapter 8 Review Questions 82
- Chapter 9: Animals and the Environment 85
  - Learning Objectives 85
  - Environmental Ethics 85
    - Anthropocentrism (Ethical Humanism) 85
    - Biocentrism (Eco-centrism) 85
  - The Land Ethic 87
- Chapter 9 Review Questions 88
- Chapter 10: Intimate Relationships, Equality, and Discrimination 89
  - Learning Objectives 89
  - Friendship 89
  - Natural Law and Sex 89
    - Nagel's Secular Philosophy 90
    - Plato 90
    - Date Rape 90
  - Equality and Discrimination 91
    - John Stuart Mill 91
    - Will Kymlicka 92
    - Richard Wasserstrom 92
- Chapter 10 Review Questions 93

Chapter 11: Affirmative Action and Free Speech 94
Learning Objectives 94
Affirmative Action 94
Free Speech 95
Pornography 99
Chapter 11 Review Questions 101
Appendix A: Overview of Ethical Theories, Theorists, and Terminology 103
Appendix B: Ethical Analysis of Issues and Practical Applications 116
Relationships and Sexuality 116
Pornography 117
Public Health 118
Ethical Decisions Surrounding Major Types of Medical Care 120
Resuscitation 120
Hospice Care 121
Defective Newborns and the Morality of Termination 124
Economic Inequity, Poverty, and Equal Opportunity 124
Racism and Affirmative Action 125
Punishment 126
Death Penalty 127
War and Peace 128
Realism 130
Pacifism 130
Terrorism 131
Biomedical Ethics: Cloning to Produce Children 131
Arguments in Favor 132
Arguments Against 132
Environmental Ethics 133
Answers for Chapter Review Questions 135
PRACTICE EXAM 136
PRACTICE EXAM ANSWER KEY 161

Preparing for Your Ethics Exam

Chances are if you are reading this, you are a student looking to perform well on an upcoming test. Congratulations, you have taken the first step in achieving that goal. Yes, you have purchased this text, but more importantly this means you have determined to seek success and do what it takes to achieve this success. This means you are already in the right mindset to begin…so why don't we do just that and get started?

Taking a test and performing well is much like a sport. Consider the test to be the "big game" that students face over and over. Every athlete knows the importance of preparing for the game through practice, drills, and training. Just preparing is not enough; the athlete also knows the rules for his or her chosen sport and has developed the ability to remain calm under pressure. Each of these three skills comes together to allow the athlete to perform to the best of their ability and hopefully win the "big game". As a student, you have no doubt heard more than once that tests are designed to demonstrate your knowledge of the subject matter, and while that is true, this is not the entire picture. We have all encountered that student who studies less than everyone yet manages to pass or even get an "A" on the tests they take. Chances are this student not only knows the subject matter, but they know how to play the game. This text is designed to help you understand those "rules" and develop skills that will make you a master test taker. This guide will in no way substitute for knowledge of subject matter, but will certainly assist you in making sure that your test accurately demonstrates that knowledge and that the "rules of the game" operate in your favor. As we move forward, we are going to analyze some study skills that will help you acquire the subject matter knowledge necessary for your test, learn a few test-taking skills that will help you "play the game" even better, and examine how to work well under pressure (relive some of the test anxiety).

Study Skills

Ask almost anyone and they will tell you that the key to success on a test is to know the subject materials for which you are being tested. As we already mentioned, this is only part of the puzzle, but it is an important part. Thus, it is where we will begin our journey together – how to best acquire this subject matter expertise. Our goal here is to help you make the most of the time you invest for studying so that you gain the most knowledge possible in the time you commit to studying.

One of the most important things you can do, as a student, is to determine your learning style. This knowledge will serve you not only for this test, but for every class you ever take. There are a myriad of online quizzes that will help you identify your learning style, but for the sake of brevity we are going to discuss the five basic learning styles here. Chances are you already know how you learn best, even if you have never formally addressed this topic. The five learning styles are described below.

1. Visual learning – has a preference for learning through pictures, graphs, and spatial understanding.
2. Auditory – sometimes called musical – learns best through sound and lectures.
3. Verbal – sometimes called linguistic – process information through words both verbal and written.
4. Kinesthetic – this learner processes by feeling, sensing, and doing
5. Logical – sometimes called mathematical – uses logic and reasoning

If you are a **visual** learner you will want to spend time making graphs, charts, timelines, maps, and pictures that will help you understand the materials. You are going to remember far more about a picture, than information you simply read. If you are an **auditory** learner, then you are one in a small percentage of students who actually do learn through the lecture model that most of western education is built upon. The auditory learner will do best by reading texts books aloud so that they are not simply reading, but hearing the text. Much like the auditory learner, the **verbal** learner should also read test materials aloud. In this case, it is not hearing the content, but in verbalizing it. In addition to spoken word, the verbal learner also learns well by writing information. This makes the practice of note-taking especially beneficial to this learner. The **kinesthetic** learner is often the most challenging for teachers and professors to address. It is the kinesthetic learner who learns best by actually "doing". If you are this type of learner then you need to feel, hold, and manipulate objects in order to best understand the content. This type of learner will learn better while moving around and seldom studies well at a typical desk. Finally, the **logical** learner needs to understand the "why" behind ideas and concepts. The logical learner needs to see connections and reasons behind the information. Memorization of facts does not typically serve the logical learner as well as a thorough understanding of how the concepts relate to one another. It is important to note here that while one primary sense is usually tied to your learning style, you should incorporate as many senses as possible into your learning routine. So for the visual learner, it is imperative that they see the information in displayed form, but they will also enhance their memory be utilizing their auditory, verbal, and kinesthetic skills. Remember the more senses you can involve in the learning process the better. Don't be afraid to draw, read aloud, sing, or create objects that can be moved in order to see the logic and connections behind the facts.

In addition to the five different learning styles, there are two additional styles that some authors have added. These two are the solitary and social learner. These two types of learners can be found in conjunction with any of the above five learning styles. For example, one could be a solitary visual learner. As the name implies, the solitary learner prefers to learn alone while the social learner prefers learning in the group setting. While the solitary learner is likely to be found alone in the library, the social learner gravitates toward study groups and enjoys group projects that the solitary learner often dreads.

There has been much debate over the years regarding the best time of day to study. The short answer is, there is no one correct answer. The best time of day for study is completely student dependent. If an individual is more alert in the morning then they should study in the morning. If the student is better in the evening, then study in the evening. Most fathers are fond of reminding their children that "you can't hoot with the owls and soar with the eagles." Of course, the preference is typically that you soar with the morning eagles and avoid the night owls as much as possible. However, the main idea serves as a great reminder for students – if you are a morning person make sure to get enough rest to rise early and make use of that time. If you are indeed a night owl, then sleep in and be sure you devote the evening time to study, not just socializing with friends.

With the preliminaries out of the way, let us dive into some more hands on considerations that will help you make the most of your study time.

1. Prepare your space –
    a. Do not study in your bed. Our bodies are conditioned to see the bed as a place of rest and relaxation. By attempting to study in bed, we are constantly fighting the ingrained habit of our bodies. In addition, it can be difficult to fight the constant temptation to take a "quick cat nap" that turns into an hour or two of lost time.
    b. If you do not study in bed, where should you study? Really just about anywhere else that works for you and fits your learning style. Consider a dedicated space that you use only for study. The more you use the space the more your brain will begin to equate the space with productive study.
    c. For most students, a desk really is the best option as it not only sets the tone for study and work but also promotes good posture. Many kinesthetic learners benefit from a standing desk or a chair that allows for movement.
    d. Consider the lighting. Select a space that has good natural light and allows for good artificial light to be added if studying at night. In seeking natural light be cautious of windows. While they do provide great natural light, they can also be a source of distraction. If possible consider this in the placement of your desk. Desks placed to the side of a window allow for good light, but the temptation to gaze into the outdoors is limited by not being situated directly in front of you.
    e. Gather all your materials. Make sure you study space is adequately stocked with all the necessary materials: books, pens and pencils, paper, computer, printer, etc.
    f. Select appropriate music. For most learning styles, music that is instrumental is best for learning. This prevents one from using

part of the brain to sing along instead of being focused on the topic at hand. For the auditory or musical learner, music can be especially powerful as subject material can be tied to the music for better understanding and recall.

2. Create a schedule for study. Determine what topics will be covered by your test and how many days you have to study for the exam. Plan out what topics you will study each day in order to be prepared for the test. Do not plan on studying any new material the night before the exam, as cramming is never a good option. Be sure to devote more time to topics that are unfamiliar or difficult.

3. Use a timer. Set your timer for 20 or 25 minutes. Studies show that the optimal time to study is in 20 to 25 minute segments with a 5 to 10 minute break between each. Your brain is actually best at remembering the first and last thing that you study. Therefore these short segments give you more first and last items. These short segments are short enough to maintain attention (even for those with ADD or ADHD) and long enough to study a substantial amount of information. During your break get up and move around. Be sure your whole body is involved. The physical activity keeps your blood flowing and gives your brain a chance to take a break, without shutting down completely.

4. Study in "chunks". As we mentioned earlier your brain is great at remembering the first and last items on which you focus attention. Use this fact to your advantage by breaking information into lists or chunks of 3 to 5 items. This allows for more first and lasts in the set of information and uses your brains built in systems to your advantage.

5. Concentrate. It seems like the simplest advice, but the importance of concentration cannot be overstated. Concentration is the self-discipline of studying. Studying is not a passive skill (as much as all students wish it was). Studying is an active sport. You must engage your brain. If you struggle with concentration or suffer from ADD / ADHD consider removing anything that might distract you. For this author this meant going to the top floor of the library where the "quite rule" was strictly

enforced, finding an enclosed study area where there were no visual distractions, and putting earplugs in so that not even the turning of pages could distract me. It soon became apparent that an hour spent in this environment was far more productive than 2 or 3 hours trying to study in a dorm room or even a more social area of the library. Do not be afraid to do what it takes to make concentration easier, it is a difficult discipline to build.

6. DO NOT use a highlighter when studying. A highlighter may be beneficial in marking items to be studied at a later time, but that is precisely what makes it such a poor tool for studying. The best use for a highlighter is in a fast paced lecture when something needs to be noted for later study. However, when studying as an individual the highlighter often serves as a mark of procrastination. Instead of highlighting the text to come back to later, take the time to devote it to memory. If the information is too in-depth or is a bit off topic, make a note on a separate piece of paper to come back and study further. The simple act of writing it down instead of highlighting begins the learning process. Make every attempt to understand and process information before moving along to another topic and instead of highlighting for later study.

7. Create connections. The more you can connect a new concept to something you already know the better your learning and recall will be. For visual learners, these connections should be drawn in pictures, flow charts or graphs. For the kinesthetic learner, as much as possible, the connections should be acted out or put into motions.

8. Use all of your senses. As much as possible try to engage all of your senses when studying. It is understood that your sight is always part of studying. Include your speech (which we know is not a true sense) and hearing in your study. Instead of just reading material silently "in your head", read it out loud. This engages three aspects of your brain: sight, hearing, and speech which make it more likely you will remember the content. If there is a way you can integrate the whole body into the concept then do so.

9. Study items from broad concepts to minor details. As you begin to study, tackle the major points first. If you understand how whole chapters relate to one another then adding the smaller details will be easier.

10. Always focus on the bold print or italicized words in a text, as these are strong indicators of important material.

11. When you study consider using the same pen / pencil for all study related to this test and then take this pencil with you to the testing center. As you study play a mental trick on yourself by storing all the answers you write into your pencil. With that pencil with you at the exam, you have already written all the answers you are going to need. Sure it is a mental trick, but you have actually studied hard and written all the answers you are going to need. The mental trick simply serves as a psychological reminder to this fact.

12. Use flash cards. Sometimes there is information that simply must be devoted to memory (formulas, historical events, lists, vocabulary). For this type of information use flash cards. Three by five index cards work well. Put the definition or name of the formula on the front of the card and the answer on the back. Quiz yourself using the cards and reviewing the cards you missed in each set before attempting to work through the entire deck again. Flash cards work great for reviewing materials when you only have a few moments (perhaps between classes, or waiting in line).

13. Use mnemonic techniques to memorize materials. There are several mnemonic techniques that work well depending on the situation.

    a. For key words or lists consider using an ACRONYM to remember the list. An acronym is an invented combination of letters. If you have ever had the pleasure of playing a musical instrument you probably remember your grade school music teacher saying Every Good Boy Does Fine in an effort to help you remember the order of the notes on the clef scale.

b. Another option for lists or key words is the ACROSTIC - You probably remember Please Excuse My Dear Aunt Sally from grade school when your teacher used it to help you remember the order of operations: Parenthesis, Exponents, Multiply, Divide, Addition, Subtraction.

c. Location method – this method involves using a specific location to tie concepts together. For this example let us assume we are trying to memorize the following short list of landforms: hill, mountain, and plateau. We might picture our living room and imagine that as we walk in the door we are met immediately by a hill we must crawl over, followed by a television displaying a picture of the mountain. Lastly sitting there on the sofa is a plateau (you may even picture your uncle who has the flat buzz cut to help you remember the flat plateau). The more vivid you make the pictures the better and easier to remember them they will be.

d. Rhyming Method – This is a two-step method in which you create words that rhyme with numbers and then build an association with those words. This method works best for ordered lists. For example if you were going to remember the following items for a grocery list: milk, bread, eggs, cheese, and chicken. To remember the first item on the list we would find a word that rhymes with "one". For our case, we will choose "run". You are going to picture yourself running and carrying a gallon of milk. Much like the Location method, the trick to making this particular mnemonic device work is to make the picture and relationship between the two words as vivid as possible. So instead of just picturing yourself running with a gallon of milk in hand, you will picture yourself running while pouring the milk over your head. You could even get some of your other senses involved by imagining the smell of the milk to be putrid due to the hot weather in which you are running. By involving more senses and making the picture more vivid you are far less likely to forget the milk when you arrive at the store. This process would be repeated using the next number in the sequence and so on for each item that needs to be memorized.

14. Study groups – If you are a social learner then you will certainly benefit from the advantages that study groups offer. However, be prepared when you arrive and do not expect the study group to replace individual effort needed to learn new material. Study groups typically work best, for both social and solitary learners as a place to test knowledge. By quizzing one another, students can become more confident about material they know and find out what concepts may need a bit more attention. In addition, study groups can often help the student who is stumped on a particular concept. Do not be afraid to ask for study group members to explain something or help you understand it more clearly. Often hearing something described in different words is just the key our brain needs to unlock the information fully.

Scheduling Your Test

It may seem like a simplistic reminder, but if you are a morning person you will want to schedule your exam for the morning hours. Be sure to give yourself adequate time to get up, get ready and face any traffic on your way to the testing center. If you are better in the evenings, schedule the time that is near the end of the day but NOT the last session. Think back to elementary school and the fear of being the last person to turn in their test while others waited for you. You do not want the added stress of those around you leaving while you needlessly fear being the only person left.

Last Minute Preparation for Testing

You have studied as much as possible and tomorrow is the big day. What should you do tonight to make sure you are prepared for the big test? Let us begin with the one thing you should NOT do. Do not get caught up in cramming or even reviewing one last time. It is actually too late for that to do you much good. Tonight you should relax and focus on just a few items.

Ethics: Theory and Practice

1. Get to bed early (or at least not excessively late) so you will be fresh for your test.

2. Use this time for positive self-talk. Remind yourself how much you have studied for this exam and how prepared you are to show just how well you know the information.

3. The night before set out the items you will need for testing. Lay out clothing you plan to wear (go for comfort over style here). Make sure you include a jacket / hoodie as most testing centers tend to stay cold to help you stay awake. In addition, be sure your photo ID, pencils, calculator, and other requirements for the test are ready to be grabbed as you walk out the door.

4. Eat breakfast. Sure this is motherly advice, but it is good advice. Your brain needs fuel to function. Make sure you feed it. Avoid sugary foods that will leave you in a slump later and impact concentration levels. High protein foods are best as they help provide long-term energy.

5. Visit the restroom 15 – 20 minutes before the test and refrain from drinking fluids within an hour of your test.

6. Arrive 10-15 minutes early for the test so you do not have the stress of being late.

7. During the last few minutes, it is okay to review a formula or fact sheet of information you have dedicated to memory. One of the first things you will do when you sit for the exam, is to "dump" this information onto your scrap paper. Note that this is not the time to "cram" this information into your brain. It should already be memorized; you are just reviewing one last time.

8. Before you are seated for the exam, take a few deep breaths and relax. If you are subject to test anxiety we will cover more on how to relax a bit later.

Test-Taking Tips

When we began this text we explained that taking a test was much like a sport and that understanding the rules of the game (test-taking skills) were just as important as ability to play (subject matter knowledge). In the next several pages we are going to explore ways you can put the rules of the game to work for you. By understanding and applying these test-taking strategies you improve your odds for success.

The number one tip for taking a test is to **remain confident**. It is amazing how confidence can change the outcome of situations. If you have studied adequately your hard work will pay off when it comes to taking the test. Just relax and trust yourself. If you suffer from test anxiety this tip is even more important. (See also the tips for test anxiety a few pages later.)

Once you begin the test and the timer begins, **take the first few moments to write down any formulas, dates, facts that you have dedicated to memory**, but are not included on a "fact sheet" for the exam. Doing this "brain dump" allows your brain to figuratively free up space that was being used to hold this information. It also ensures you do not forget the information later down the road when you need it.

Before you begin, take a look at the entire test and determine how you will **budget your time**. Often tests are computerized so this does not mean to click through every question, but simply learning how many questions there are so that you can stay on target to finish in the time allotted.

It often goes without saying, but it should not, that you need to **read the instructions**. You have probably had that teacher that gave you the following directions test that asked you to read the whole test before marking any answers and the result likely resulted in hilarity as your classmates did silly things because they didn't read the directions. (You would never fall for that trick yourself). While this is not elementary school and a standardized test is not going to set out to confuse you with directions, they are no less important. The difference between understanding mark the "best" answer and "only" answer can save you a great deal of confusion, and the difference between writing an essay about all of the topics or choosing a topic can mean the difference in passing and failing. So as elementary and boring as it is, take time to read the directions.

After reading the directions, you will want to **begin with the easiest questions** first. Most tests today are written in increased order of difficulty so this is typically the way you approach the test anyway. Answering easy questions will serve to boost your self-confidence and prepare you for the harder questions to come. However, if you encounter a problem that "stumps" you do not be afraid to leave it unanswered and return to it at a later time. Be sure you either mark the question on the test or make note on your scrap paper so you do not submit the test with an unanswered question. A question may often have clues to other questions within it.

As you answer questions **rely on your first impressions** and do not over think the answers. Unless you are 100% sure that you have the wrong answer and are 100% that the answer you are changing to is the correct answer do not deviate from your initial "gut reaction". Teachers would be quite wealthy if rewarded every time a student admitted to changing from a correct to incorrect answer. Do not be that student. Go with your first instincts unless you are absolutely sure you were wrong.

If you finish early, **use the time to review** your answers. Check to be sure you answered all of the questions. Proofread any essays for spelling and grammatical errors. If the test covered mathematics, check your calculations and use the calculator if it is acceptable to do so.

Multiple Choice Questions

Depending on the type of test you are likely to encounter different types of questions. Each of these question types has specific strategies that will help you in taking tests. The most common type of test question for standardized tests is the **multiple-choice** test. Consider these strategies for these types of questions:

1. Before reading the answers to a multiple-choice question try to formulate the answer on your own. This adds confidence to your answer and ensures your brain is engaged in the answering process.
2. While you should formulate your own answer before reading the choices, be sure you read all of the answers before selecting your answer.
3. Statements that begin with concrete exceptions: never, none, always, except, most, least, are likely not the answer.
4. Eliminate unlikely answers. If you can reduce the possible answers to 2 you increase your odds of selecting the right answer or even guessing correctly.
5. If you must guess consider these guidelines:

Ethics: Theory and Practice

    a. If there are two answers that are opposites from one another than the answer is likely one of those two answers.

    b. If there are two answers that are very similar, it is likely that the answer is neither of the two.

    c. Typically the longer and more descriptive answer is the correct answer

    d. If your answers are numbers then it is likely that the answer lies in the middle of the range of answers, not at the extremes. For example, if you answers are:

    a) 100   b) 10   c) 9   d) 0.02

You would eliminate the 100 and .02 and then determine if the answer is either 9 or 10. Again this is not always correct but helps in a situation where you may be forced to guess.

6. Be sure you answer every question. Most tests do not penalize you for guessing so it is best to answer every question even if guessing. Research your specific test for rules about penalties for wrong answers so you know how to approach guessing.

7. Watch out for questions that ask for opposites such as "which of the following is NOT" or "Which statement is false." These questions require reverse thinking.

True / False Questions

While it is not common for Standardized test to have questions other than multiple choice sometimes you may encounter True / False questions. For **True / False** questions consider the following tips:

1. Look at specific details. Specific details tend to make the statement true. For example, The Empire State Building is 1,250 feet tall. The detail of 1250 feet is a very specific detail and chances are this test question is TRUE.

2. When forced to guess, choose TRUE. More questions tend to be true than false, as most instructors and test writers find it more difficult to write statements that are false.

3. Look for extreme words such as: all, always, only, nobody, everybody, absolutely, etc. These words tend be used in statements that are FALSE.

4. Look for qualifying words such as: seldom, often, many, seldom, much, sometimes, etc. These words tend to make the statement TRUE.

5. Look for reasons. If the statement includes a reason it tends to be FALSE. Words like since, because, when, and if add justification or reasoning to the statement and tend to make it FALSE. Also check the justification to make sure it is complete. An incomplete justification makes the statement FALSE.

6. Look for negative words such as: not, none, or no. Also check for negative prefixes such as *un-, im-, miss-*. These negatives can confuse the statement and should be treated with caution.

Matching Questions

Sometimes you will encounter matching questions. These will often appear in a format very similar to multiple choice questions, but should be treated a bit differently. Here are a few tips to help you navigate these types of questions.

1. Read the directions carefully. Sometimes matching answers may be used only once, in other questions the answers may be used more than once. This certainly makes guessing much more difficult if there are answers that can be used more than once.

2. Look at both "sides" or sets of answers / questions. Get an idea of what the relationships might be between the two groups.

3. Use one list to find matches on the second list. This will keep confusion to a minimum.

4. Check the entire second "side" before selecting answers. There may be a more correct answer that follows.

5. Cross off matches on the second "side" in order to make finding subsequent matches easier.

6. Do not make a guess until you have worked through the entire first "side" one time completely.

Ethics: Theory and Practice

Essay Questions

Some of the standardized test you will be taking may include essay questions. The approach to these tests is quite different from that of multiple choice or true-false exams as it is not really possible to guess at answers. When you answer essay questions you should remember that the idea is to show how well you both know the material and can explain it. You should also provide support for your answer. As you answer Essay Questions keep these tips in mind.

1. Read the entire question before beginning to write.
2. Construct a brief outline with the main points before you begin writing. If you are suffering from writers block then just begin by jotting down the ideas that come to mind. Even if you do not physically write out the outline, you should develop the main ideas in your head and have a distinct direction before you begin your writing.
3. Remember these tips for a good answer:
a. Be direct in the answer to the question. Pose the answer in the first or second sentence of your answer.
b. Make sure to include both general and specific information.
c. Use vocabulary that is common to the course you are testing. If you are taking an ethics test, use the language of ethics.
4. Proofread your paper. Check for spelling, grammar, and punctuation. Also, make sure that your answer completely answers the question at hand and covers the entire problem. Be sure that your essay is easy to read and makes sense or flows well.
5. Monitor your time on an essay question. Time management is imperative in completion of the essay type question.

Overcoming Test Anxiety

One of the most debilitating problems a student can face is test anxiety. Test anxiety can manifest itself through tense muscles, fast heart and breathing rate, cramps, and even nausea. The student who suffers from test anxiety often knows the material as well as, or better than his or her classmates, but this never shows up on tests because the anxiety takes over. It is important for those who suffer from test anxiety to remain calm and confident. There are also other ways to help the brain and body cope with this type of anxiety.

1. **Breathe**. Breathing is not only essential to our existence, but serves as a way of relaxing the mind and body. Purposefully taking a few deep breaths can do a great deal to bring calm to the body. When you feel anxiety about to take over, begin to breathe deeply and calmly. Three to five deep breaths normally do the trick and can be repeated as often as necessary.

2. **Relax**. There will be times during the test that you begin to feel anxious. Recognize this feeling. Does it begin with tightening of the shoulders and neck or does it start in your stomach and slowly take over your body? Become aware of the feelings and the how they start. When you feel that trigger or beginning feeling consciously focus on relaxation. There are many great books and websites dedicated to relaxation techniques. Explore and find one that works best for you.

3. **Take practice tests.** Before you sit for the actual exam, take as many practice exams as you can. Make the surroundings as much like the test center as you can. Give yourself the same time limits, and breaks you will be taking during the exam. The more you can make the practice seem like a test, the more the test will seem like practice. This brings us to the next point.

4. **Think of the test as practice**. This author, once had a student who scored a 32 on a quiz that covered multiplication facts all of which the student had recited the day before. It was apparent the student had become more and more anxious during the exam. As the class was assigned a new worksheet, this student was given the same quiz with one slight change made. At the top of the page, the word "Quiz" was replaced by "Practice". Guess what he made on the "Practice" sheet? You guessed it; he made a 100. Sure it is going to be hard to convince yourself that the test you are going to take at a testing center is really a "Practice" sheet, but there is no reason that you cannot retake the test. Most CLEP and standardized tests allow you to reset for the exam in 6

months (some less). Sure that is a while to wait and you do not want to stress over this test again, but remind yourself this is not the only shot you have at this. Take some of the pressure off of yourself.

5. **Do not panic**. Chances are that if you suffer from test anxiety you are already well acquainted with panic. Simply do not give into it. Force yourself to relax while reminding yourself of your confidence through positive self-talk.

6. **Stay Positive.** Remind yourself of how much you are prepared for this and that a poor exam score only results from many missed questions not one or two.

7. **Stay Realistic.** As we just mentioned one wrong answer does not mean you will fail the exam. Remind yourself that you simply need to pass. No one needs to know your score; you just need to do well enough to pass the exam. As you continue with positive self-talk do not let one or two questions send you into a spiral of self-doubt and more anxiety. Stay realistic about outcomes and your performance.

8. **Take care of yourself**. This is the most often overlooked advice when it comes to test anxiety. Your body is much more likely to respond appropriately if you are treating it appropriately by eating healthy foods and exercising regularly. In addition, regular exercise is shown to reduce stress and is a great way to build up tolerance and coping skills for test anxiety.

As you prepare for your upcoming exam, realized there are no shortcuts to doing well on a test. There is no replacement for knowledge of this subject matter, but hopefully the study skills mentioned here will help you make the most of your time spent studying. As you take the test remember the test- taking skills, as these will help you demonstrate your true mastery of the subject matter. Before you set for the exam and anxiety takes over be sure to put into practice some of the tactics we have mentioned for overcoming anxiety. If you already know what techniques work well for you those techniques will be at your disposal during the test.

Remember that just as the athlete must not only has mastery of the sport but must understand the rules and remain calm under pressure so must you the test-taker. It is important that you master all three skills as each plays a part in your success. You may not be scoring goals, sinking baskets, or serving aces, but you are going to win this game called test-taking. Just remember to have confidence in yourself.

Ethics: Theory and Practice

Introduction to your text:

This text prepares you to take the Excelsior College *Ethics: Theory and Practice* examination. This exam measures ethical knowledge as it applies to practical ethical situations. Application of knowledge about ethics is accomplished through the use of case studies and related sets of multiple-choice questions. Knowledge categories include basic theories and concepts such as utilitarianism, natural law theory, justice, duties and obligations, and rights.

General Course Objectives:

1. Identify key attributes, strengths, and weaknesses associated with ethical theories such as natural law, the social contract, deontology, utilitarianism, virtue ethics, egoism, intuitionism, feminism, and existentialism.
2. Distinguish among basic concepts such as justice, rights, values, goods, duties, obligations, morals, and autonomy.
3. Identify and differentiate among meta-ethical concepts.
4. Identify and differentiate among principles of moral deliberation.
5. When given a case study involving social and personal issues, medical issues, professional and business issues, or environmental issues, demonstrate the ability to:
6. Identify applications of ethical theories
7. Evaluate person's course of action based on his or her ethical principles and knowledge base.
8. Identify differences and similarities in moral arguments. Recognize common logical fallacies in a moral argument. Evaluate judgments in terms of basic concepts.

Chapter 1: Ethics and Ethical Reasoning

Learning Objectives
After reading this chapter, you should be able to:

1. Differentiate between ethics and morality.
2. Define deontological ethics, teleological ethics, and virtue ethics.
3. Differentiate between normative ethics and non-normative ethics.
4. Differentiate between moral judgments and non-moral judgments.
5. Identify the components of a valid argument and logical fallacies.

What is Morality?

The word morality comes from the Latin root *mos*, meaning "custom." The terms *morality* and *ethics* are often used interchangeably, and both words are broadly defined as having to do with right and wrong. However, there is a difference: morality is used to refer to moral standards and moral conduct, while ethics is used to refer to the formal study of those standards and conduct. For this reason, the study of ethics is also known as "moral philosophy."

What is Ethics?

The word ethics comes from the Greek root *ethos*, meaning "character." Ethics is a branch of philosophy that seeks to address questions about morality. These questions include how moral values should be determined (normative ethics), what moral values people actually abide by (descriptive ethics), how to use ethics in "real-life situations" (applied ethics), and the meaning of ethical terms, judgments, and arguments (meta-ethics).

Ethics is a topic that transcends gender, race, monetary statue, or any other symbol to help determine the nature of people and the purpose of their actions and thought processes. Do ethics follow law, religious beliefs, or societal norms? Many have come before and many will come after asking *"Why?"* For this reason, it is imperative to question, ponder, and then, answer this question, in order to understand the structure of the lives we choose to live.

There are two main approaches for studying ethics: normative ethics (ethical theory and applied ethics) and non-normative ethics (descriptive/meta-ethics).

Normative Ethics

The term *normative* reflects the ordinary view that some things are better than others. It is used when making judgments that involve basic values and is based on cultural norms. Normative ethics has three branches: virtue ethics, deontological ethics, and teleological ethics.

Virtue Ethics places an emphasis on who you are rather than what you do. Morality stems from the identity and/or character of the individual, rather than being a reflection of the actions of the individual. The basis of virtue ethics lies in the belief that in order to live a moral life one must begin by developing good character. We, therefore, ought to act in ways that exhibit virtues (such as courage or compassion) even if that means doing what might generally be seen as bad or bringing about undesirable consequences. For example, exercising the virtue of courage to be a whistleblower, even if it means losing one's job or causing others to lose their jobs is considered both virtuous and undesirable. Another example might be of someone exercising patience and restraint even if it means losing out on an opportunity.

Deontological ethics comes from the Greek words for duty (*deon*) and science (*logos*). This "science of duty" approach focuses on the rightness or wrongness of motives. It is also described as duty- or obligation-based ethics because deontologists believe that ethical rules bind you to your duty. These duties or obligations are usually determined by God; therefore, being moral is often a matter of obeying God.

Divine Command Theory is an example of a deontological theory. It actually refers to a cluster of related theories that state an action is right if God has decreed that it is right. The basic tenet is that God's will is the basis of morality.

Teleological ethics derives its name from the Greek word for "purpose," *telos*. This type of ethics focuses on the consequences that an action may have, and are often referred to as **Consequentialist** moral systems. In teleological ethics, acts are justified by demonstrating that the moral behind the act fits into some larger purpose. To make correct moral choices, we must have some understanding of what will result from our choices. If our actions result in correct consequences, we are acting morally. If our actions result in incorrect consequences, we are acting immorally. The action is not the focus; rather, maximizing good results is the focus.

Utilitarianism is one example of a Consequentialist moral theory. At the core of utilitarianism is the **Principle of Utility** or the **Greatest Happiness Principle**. An ethical decision is one that offers the greatest net utility: the greatest amount of happiness for the greatest number of people.

Non-Normative Ethics

While normative ethics are based on evaluative judgments, deeming one thing better or more desirable than another, non-normative ethics, also known as **descriptive ethics** is based on objective judgments, made from quantifiable data. The factual investigation of the logic, language, and objectivity of moral systems, non-normative ethics often employs empirical and experimental data from other disciplines such as sociology, psychology, or history. While normative ethics deal with personal beliefs, non-normative ethics focuses on factual beliefs. "Spanking is (or is not) justified" is an example of a normative judgment. "Spanking does (or does not) modify behavior effectively," is an example of a non-normative judgment. It is a **descriptive statement** (also known as an **empirical judgment**) about the world that relies on experimental or empirical information.

Comparative ethics is a type of descriptive ethics that studies people's beliefs about morality. It describes how people behave and/or what sorts of moral standards they claim to follow.

Meta-ethics is also known as **analytic ethics**. In philosophy, meta-ethics is the branch of ethics that seeks to understand the nature of ethical properties (if there are any), and ethical statements, attitudes, and judgments. Whenever a moral system is created, it is based upon certain premises about reality, human nature, values, etc. Meta-ethics questions the validity of those premises and argues that maybe we don't really know what we are talking about after all! It is distinct from normative ethics because in meta-ethics we are not trying to figure out what we <u>ought</u> to do. Rather, we are trying to figure out what it means to say we <u>ought</u> to do something. *A more extensive discussion of meta-ethics and its related theories will follow in chapter 2.*

Moral Judgments, Argumentation, and Reasoning

People frequently give arguments about the right action, but when asked to explain why they think something is or is not good or right, they answer, "It just is." This isn't very convincing, unless the person you are talking to happens to already agree with you. Being able to say why we think that something is good or right in a way that is convincing to other is one goal of ethical discussions.

While reasoning and arguing it is important to understand the types of **judgments** used in the process. **Moral judgments** are normative judgments that presume a moral norm or standard. As discussed above, **normative** (or **evaluative**) **judgments** are based on the moral values of society at the time.

Ethics: Theory and Practice

As societal values change, normative judgments change. **Value judgments** are types of normative judgments that something is good or bad, or that one thing is better or worse than something else. **Prescriptive judgments** or statements are normative judgments that attempt to regulate or guide behavior through the use of terms such as *ought* and *shouldn't*.

In order to discuss ethical questions with people of differing positions, you need to learn to argue effectively. The objective of learning the basics of **argumentation** are 1) to speak convincingly to support your point, perhaps to change the mind of your opposition, and 2) to be able to recognize faulty reasoning that often obscures the true issue(s) at hand.

Argumentation: Basic Terms and Concepts

Premise: a statement about something known or assumed, which forms the basis of an argument, and is the idea supported by the reasoning in the argument. It can also be called a **proposition**. In writing a paper, it would be the *thesis*.

Assumption: Something taken for granted; a supposition. Synonyms for assumption are
presupposition, hypothesis, conjecture, guess, postulate, theory.

Argument: The combination of one or more premises and a conclusion. It is also a process of reasoning that begins with a premise and ends with a conclusion.

Sound argument: A valid argument with a true premise, thus a sound argument has a true conclusion.

Counter example: An exception to a proposed general rule usually used to argue that a certain philosophical position is wrong by showing that it does not apply in certain cases.

Logical Fallacy: An error of reasoning, which is the opposite of a sound argument. When someone adopts a position, or tries to persuade someone else to adopt a position, based on a faulty piece of reasoning, he/she commits a fallacy. Some common fallacies include:

Slippery slope: Asserting that if we allow A to happen, then Z will consequently happen too, therefore A should not happen.

Straw man: Misrepresenting someone's argument to make it easier to attack.

False dilemma: Two alternative states are presented as the only possibilities, when other possibilities exist. (Also known as "black-or-white" or "either/or" fallacy.)

Appeal to Nature: Making the argument that because something is "natural" it is therefore valid, justified, inevitable, or ideal, or alternatively, because something is "unnatural" it is harmful of undesirable. (Also known as "Naturalistic" fallacy.)

Ad Hominem: Attacking your opponent's character or personal traits instead of engaging with their argument.

Bandwagon: Appealing to the popularity or the fact that many people do something as a form of validation for it.

Other types of fallacies include: False cause, special pleading, begging the question, appeal to authority, appeal to emotion, poisoning the well, genetic fallacy, confusing cause and effect, burden of proof, biased sample, hasty generalization, guilt by association, etc.

Ethics: Theory and Practice

Chapter 1 Review Questions

Read the scenarios and answer the questions that follow. Scenario 1:

There is a homeless man on the street holding a sign that reads "Hungry- can you help?" and a cup with change. I put a five-dollar bill into the cup and tell him to buy a sandwich.

1. If I did this because I believe it was my duty to help the less-privileged, my action represents
    a. Teleological ethics
    b. Deontological ethics
    c. Virtue ethics
    d. Non-normative ethics
2. If I did this because I believe that exercising compassion to other people is important, my action represents
    a. Teleological ethics
    b. Deontological ethics
    c. Virtue ethics
    d. Non-normative ethics
3. If I did this because I believe that helping the less-privileged improves society, my action represents
    a. Teleological ethics
    b. Deontological ethics
    c. Virtue ethics
    d. Non-normative ethics

Scenario 2:

A school institutes a new identification card policy in which all students and staff, at all times, must wear a school picture ID card on a lanyard around their necks. Students will not be allowed into the school building without their IDs and cannot attend any school activities without it.
The administrators explain to the student body that the new rule is to address safety concerns. There had been several instances where students from other schools had come to the building to begin altercations with students. The new policy is to help keep out people who do not belong in

the school, and to signal to teachers and administrators that those people wearing the IDs belonged in the school.

    4. By explaining the reason for the new rule, the administrators are demonstrating an adherence to
- a. Teleological ethics
- b. Deontological ethics
- c. Virtue ethics
- d. Non-normative ethics

Scenario 3:

Several professors are meeting at the local coffee house to discuss the news of the day. Professor W begins by speaking about the conviction of a serial murderer. The murderer had killed over twenty people, including children. Professor W, who does not normally support the death penalty, feels that under these circumstances, the penalty is justified. Professor X asks what she means by "justified." Professor Y looks up the statistics to see whether states with death penalty laws have fewer murders to determine the efficacy of the death penalty. Professor Z then asks how we decide that a person who murders multiple people deserves a harsher punishment than a person who murders only one person if we are a society that values all human life equally.

    1. These professors are employing_____ in their discussion.
- e. Teleological ethics
- f. Deontological ethics
- g. Virtue ethics
- h. Non-normative ethics

Chapter 2: Ethical Relativism and Meta-ethics

Learning Objectives
After reading this chapter, you should be able to:

1. Explain the theory of ethical relativism and its criticisms.
2. Distinguish between meta-ethical ideas.
3. Identify weaknesses of meta-ethical positions.
4. Compare moral objectivism to moral subjectivism.

Ethical Relativism

Moral relativism refers to many different ideas concerning diversity of moral judgment across time, societies, and individuals. **Relativism** is the theory that the truth is different for different people. **Ethical relativism** states that what is morally right or wrong may vary fundamentally from person to person or culture to culture. It is supported by the absence of one universal morality in the modern world. Culture influences the formation of morality, and culture is a subjective phenomenon; therefore, its products can't be universal. Furthermore, the concept of **moral pluralism** suggests that there are several values which may be equally correct and fundamental, and yet in conflict with each other. Ethical relativism comes in two forms:

Personal or individual relativism states that ethical judgments and beliefs are the expression of the moral attitudes of each individual person. No one person is more correct than another since right and wrong are based on personal beliefs. Morality does not expand further than the opinion of the individual on the issues. This is an ethical **subjectivist** view, because moral values are dependent on a will, human or divine. In this view, individual conscience is the only appropriate standard for moral judgment. To an ethical subjectivist, all the power of defining an act as moral or immoral belongs to the individual.

Social or cultural relativism states that ethical values vary from one society to another. In order to decide what is morally correct, one must consult the moral beliefs of the society to which they belong. It is based on the **dependency thesis** which states that what is moral is dependent upon human nature, the human condition, and/or specific social and cultural circumstances. Ethical relativism can be discussed from two positions: descriptive and prescriptive. **Descriptive relativism** notes that there are differences among ethical practices and standards of different cultures, without evaluation of their justification. It is based on empirical fact. **Prescriptive relativism** goes further and claims that people ought not to apply the standards of one culture to evaluate the behavior of another culture.

Support for Ethical Relativism

Support for ethical relativism usually centers around three reasoned arguments:

1. **The diversity of moral views** among people and cultures is well documented through history, anthropology, science, and other related disciplines. Philosophers have disagreed about the basis of morality since ancient times, and no universal agreement has ever been reached.
2. **Moral uncertainty** in us and in our society is the second reason supporting relativism. We do not trust our own judgment, constantly questioning ourselves about the right thing to do. Do we tell the truth or do we protect a loved one? Even after making a decision, we often wonder if we made the right choice.
3. **Situational differences** between people vary so much that it is difficult to believe that the same things that would be right for one person would be right for another in all instances. Some people live in dire circumstances where basic needs such as food, water, shelter, and security are practically non-existent, while others live in comfortable circumstances where those necessities are plentiful. Some people live in oppressive societies where basic freedoms are denied, while others enjoy broad freedoms. Are the choices made by the person struggling for survival judged by the same moral compass as the person who lives comfortably and securely?

Criticisms of Relativism

Non-relativism is the converse of relativism. It has two major forms: objectivism and absolutism.

1. **Objectivism** holds there are ethical standards that are either ordained by God or by some natural moral law of the universe. Also called **universalism**, it supposes the existence of the fundamental moral principles that are correct everywhere and suitable for all people in similar situations. These moral principles are valid rules of action that should generally be adhered to, but may be overridden by other moral principles in cases of conflict. An objective value, such as health, would be universal. However, because different people have different health

needs, different moral conclusions would be made. Insulin injections are good for the diabetic, but not good for the non-diabetic. Additionally, seeming moral disagreements can be based on differing factual beliefs, which lead to differing moral conclusions. For example, people can agree on the moral value of not doing harm, but disagree on whether GMOs in food in fact causes harm; these people who share the same moral values will come to different moral conclusions on whether GMOs should be used in food production. These people disagree about what the right thing to do is, but they both believe there *is* a right thing to do, based on a universal moral value.

2. **Absolutism** differs from objectivism in that there is no exception made for situational differences or factual beliefs. To the absolutist, morals and principles are independent of context. It matters not whether a person is starving; to the absolutist, stealing food is wrong and never justified. Where the objectivist may see stealing the food as justified because it supports a good (life) which may be a greater good than property, the absolutist makes no distinction and sees it as wrong in all cases. The fundamental rules of morality are the same for all rational beings at all times and places. They do not depend on human nature, the human condition, or any specific social or cultural circumstances. There exists one moral principle and it must never be violated. Some who criticize non-relativistic thinking sometimes confuse objectivism with absolutism; however, rejecting absolutist thinking does not automatically put one in opposition with objectivist thinking.

Other Meta-ethical Theories

Philosophers in the 1900s examined moral claims through the ethical theories of **intuitionism**, **emotivism**, and **naturalism**. These theories attempt to explain the mean behind claims such as right, ought, and good.

1. **Intuitionism** makes three claims: (1) "good" is indefinable, (2) there are objective moral truths, and (3) the basic moral truths are self-evident to a mature mind. In intuitionism, we use our own intuition to find out what is right or wrong; this makes justification a private matter.
2. **Emotivism** is a non-cognitive theory where value judgments, including moral judgments, do not state facts, but are expressions of emotions or attitudes. It analyzes moral judgments as expressions of unfavorable or favorable emotion. This is an example of a **subjectivist** moral system.
3. **Naturalism** includes any belief that the nature of ethical thinking is

exhaustively understood in terms of natural tendencies of human beings, without mysterious intuitions, operations of conscience, or divine help. The natural sciences (physical or social) are used in making ethical statements, and the findings of those sciences answer ethical questions. Additionally, it suggests that our moral knowledge can be increased though our inquiry into the natural world. Naturalism is an example of a **moral realism** theory.

There are many other meta-ethical theories, and each has a theory in opposition as well.

1. **Non-naturalism** stands in opposition to naturalism. It states that moral properties exist but are not derived from natural properties. The intuitionist, G.E. Moore, combats naturalism with the **naturalistic fallacy**. He states that a naturalistic fallacy is committed whenever a philosopher attempts to prove a claim about ethics by using a definition of the term *good* in terms of natural properties (such as "pleasant" or "desired"). Moore attacks this with the **open question argument** stating that *good* is indefinable and a non-natural property.
2. **Moral realism** claims that some moral statements are objectively true. **Moral anti-realism** states there are no normative truths about one morally ought or ought not to do.
3. **Cognitivist anti-realism** is the view that all moral statements are false. **Non-cognitivist anti-realism** is the view that moral statements are neither true nor false.

Ethics: Theory and Practice

Chapter 2 Review Questions

Read the following statements. Answer the questions that follow.

Rev. L: "Abortion is wrong in any circumstance. It is the willful ending of a life, and preserving life is a universal value that must always be upheld."

Sen. B: "Abortion is wrong and should not be performed, except in cases where the life of the mother is in imminent danger. Preserving the life of the mother is the only value that would supersede the preservation of the life of the unborn."

Dr. P: "Whether or not to have an abortion is a question that each woman must decide for herself, depending on her circumstances and her own religious beliefs. The decision is an individual one and cannot be made by others."

Prof. X: "Miscarriages are spontaneous abortions that occur as a biological function to correct a medical problem. Since they occur naturally, they cannot be morally wrong. We can then extend the idea that medical abortions, when performed for medical reasons, are not morally wrong."

Judge Z: "In places where there is over-population, high poverty rates, overflowing orphanages, and famine, abortion is an accepted practice for unwanted or problem pregnancies. In places where there is reasonable population growth, low poverty rates, effective foster care and adoption services, and a high standard of living, abortion has less acceptance."

1. The person speaking from a **personal or individual ethical relativist** perspective is
    a. Rev. L
    b. Sen. B
    c. Dr. P
    d. Prof. X
    e. Judge Z
2. The person speaking from a **social or cultural relativist** perspective is
    a. Rev. L
    b. Sen. B
    c. Dr. P
    d. Prof. X
    e. Judge Z

3. The person speaking from an **ethical objectivist** perspective is
    a. Rev. L
    b. Sen. B
    c. Dr. P
    d. Prof. X
    e. Judge Z
4. The person speaking from an **ethical absolutist** perspective is
    a. Rev. L
    b. Sen. B
    c. Dr. P
    d. Prof. X
    e. Judge Z
5. The person speaking from a **ethical naturalistic** perspective is
    a. Rev. L
    b. Sen. B
    c. Dr. P
    d. Prof. X
    e. Judge Z

Ethics: Theory and Practice

Chapter 3: Egoism, Contractarianism, and Utilitarianism

Learning Objectives
After reading this chapter, you should be able to:

1. Differentiate between psychological and ethical egoism.
2. Identify strengths and weaknesses of utilitarianism and contractarianism.
3. Contrast egoism and utilitarianism.
4. Distinguish between act and rule utilitarianism.
5. Describe John Rawls's A Theory of Justice and Fairness.

Egoism

Plato uses the myth, *The Ring of Gyges*, to illustrate the concept of morality and egoism in his book *The Republic*. In *The Ring of Gyges*, a shepherd named Gyges finds a magical ring that can make him invisible. Gyges uses this power to seduce the queen and murder the king. Glaucon, the narrator, asks whether we would, like the shepherd, pursue our own interests selfishly since there would be no way of getting caught. Glaucon argues that all persons are egoistic and selfish. The only reason people do not always do the unjust thing is the fear of being caught and/or harmed.

Altruism is the opposite of egoism. Altruism is the moral obligation to benefit others rather than oneself.

There are two variants of egoism:

1. **Psychological egoism** describes human nature as being completely self-motivated and self-centered. Also called descriptive egoism, it claims that people always act selfishly, to benefit their own happiness or self-interest.
2. One type of psychological egoism is **rational egoism**. It claims that actions are rational only if they promote self-interest. The most notable proponent of rational egoism is Ayn Rand, whose writing *The Virtue of Selfishness* outlines the theory.

Strong rational egoism states that not only is it rational to pursue one's individual interests, but it is irrational not to pursue them. **Weak rational egoism** holds that while pursuing one's own interests is, in fact, rational, there may be circumstances where not pursuing them may not be considered irrational.

Ethics: Theory and Practice

Critics of psychological egoism claim that it is impossible to prove what motivates people to behave the way they do in all instances. Is the satisfaction gained from doing something for someone else the by-product of the action or the purpose of doing the action? According to the theory, we <u>always</u> act in our own self-interest; it is not enough to show that people <u>often</u> act to promote their own interests.

Ethical egoism is the normative theory that the promotion of self-interests in accordance with morality is best. People ought to do what is in their own good. **Individual ethical egoism** states that one ought to be concerned only with one's interests, and one should be concerned about others only to the extent that the concern contributes to one's interests. **Universal ethical egoism** holds that everyone ought to look out for and seek after their own best interests, helping others only when it is in their own best interests to do so.

Contractarianism

Another normative moral theory that can be considered a form of egoism is **Contractarianism**. The term applies to moral theories that focus on self-interest and denote a real or hypothetical agreement between a group and its members. All members of a society are assumed to agree to the terms of the social contract by their choice to stay within the society. Moral norms get their normative power from this mutual agreement. The best social rules are those we would accept if we chose rationally. The context in which we choose is society, so each person must make his/her choices depending on what others will do and in cooperation with them. Contractarians feel that moral and political authority should not be automatically grounded in concepts such as divine will or faith in the goodness of human nature.

Social Contract Theory was introduced by **Jean-Jacques Rousseau** in 1762, advancing ideas from Hobbes and Locke, who preceded him. According to Rousseau, a person who does what is in his/her own highest interest is doing what he/she wants. A person who does what he/she wants is free. In organized human society, there are times when our interests and wants are in conflict. Therefore, because we value our lives, we sign the Social Contract and obey it until our lives are threatened by it. A society geared to do what is best will retain everyone's freedoms (in slightly different forms), which are enjoyed so perfectly in the state of Nature. He held that society, which was created through a first, unanimous contract, carries the true will of the people, the **General Will**. The General Will is distinct from the State, a product of a majority vote, which can only give us the Will of All. Therefore, the General Will is nothing other than the repository of everyone's free choice. If forced to conform to it, a person is only forced to be free.

The idea of the social contract was revived in the 20th century by the philosopher **John Rawls**, who was concerned with the issue of fairness and social justice. He believed in a system in which social cooperation is followed by a form of established government. In advance, the members of this hypothetical society are to decide what is acceptable, determining the principles of justice. To remain objective, people should aspire to make choices for society as if behind a **veil of ignorance**, a state of naïveté which prevents them from knowing their own social and economic positions in society, which allows for judgments that are impartial. This would prevent each party from choosing the principles of justice that only benefitted themselves. Rawls' principles of fairness will be discussed in Chapter 4.

Utilitarianism

Utilitarianism is a consequentialist (goal-based) theory of ethics. It is a normative theory designed to tell us what we should do, to follow the set of rules that results in the best **consequences**. It states that the best consequences are those involving the least pain or unhappiness and the most possible pleasure or happiness.

The Utilitarian Theorists

A utilitarian is someone who accepts the principle of utility and whose concern is maximizing the value and utility of the universe.

Jeremy Bentham was a **psychological hedonist**. He believed that the desire for pleasure and aversion of pain were the only motivation for human actions. He defended the principle of utility and did not promote selfishness. The **principle of utility** states that an action is right if it produces at least as much (or more) or an increase in the happiness of all affected by it that any alternative action. An action is wrong if it does not. The principle of utility's **core beliefs** are:

1. Pleasure and happiness have intrinsic value.
2. Conversely, pain and suffering have no intrinsic value.
3. All other outcomes only have value based on whether or not they cause happiness or prevent suffering. This type of value is referred to as either instrumental or extrinsic value because it represents usefulness as a means to an end—with that end being intrinsic

value.

Bentham created the **hedonic calculus** to calculate the best or right course of action. The hedonic calculus measures **hedons**, which are units of pleasure. To use the hedonic calculus, one should measure or estimate the following seven aspects of the proposed action and its expected consequences:

1. Intensity – How intense is the pleasure/pain? Duration – How long will the pleasure/pain last? Propinquity – How soon will it occur?
2. Certainty – How likely is it to occur?
3. Fecundity – How probable is the action to produce more pleasure?
4. Purity – Will the pleasure be mixed with pain?
5. Extent – How many people will be affected?

According to this formula, a right act is the one that produces the most pleasure of all possible acts in a given situation. An act that results in an increase of pleasure is good; acts that produce more pain than pleasure are bad.

John Stuart Mill basically agreed with Bentham. He also proposed that the best thing to do is maximize happiness/utility/pleasure (which also involves minimizing unhappiness/ disutility/ pain). His goal was to find the greatest happiness for the greatest number. The main difference between the two is that Bentham judges pleasures only in terms of his seven factors; Mill, however, thinks some kinds of happiness were innately greater than others, as was shown by people favoring one over the other.

In his work *On Liberty*, Mill defended Bentham and Utilitarianism. Mill did not want society to live under a contract, but he acknowledged that people in a society should be grateful for the protection that is given, and therefore certain conduct is expected. He was a staunch proponent of **individual rights**. He believed that people should avoid harm to others as they go about their business. If one takes an action that harms others, then society should take control of the situation. This is called the **Harm Principle**, which for Mill is the only justification for the limitation of liberty. Mill did not support selfish indifference.

Mill also argued that **free speech** is crucial to the greatest happiness for the greatest number. He thought that restricting free speech prevented knowledge, and that happiness can only be achieved through knowledge. Free speech was necessary to promote knowledge and learning.

Utilitarian Justification

Utilitarian justifications are forward-looking (consequentialistic) in nature. All the questions about the justification of punishment (general justification, title, and severity) will be answered by appeal to the utility (value) of the consequences of an action. All punishment is, according to the utilitarian, <u>intrinsically</u> bad. This is because it involves the infliction of pain, or some other consequence normally considered unpleasant. Thus a system of punishment is justified only by its consequences.

Systems of punishment are usually claimed to reduce crime by three means: deterrence, incapacitation, and rehabilitation. One must also evaluate punishment on utilitarian grounds by asking certain questions about effectiveness and rationale.

The main **criticism of utilitarianism** is the argument that there is more to ethics than happiness, and that, regardless of the consequences, some things are just right or wrong. Since consequentialism determines moral rightness solely based on the consequences, it denies the influence of circumstances or the intrinsic nature of the act or anything that happens before the act. Another criticism of utilitarianism is how to determine what will make people happy. In order to apply utilitarian theory to real world situations one would need to know the exact outcome of any action, how it would affect every person involved, and what "happiness" means to each.

Subtypes of Utilitarianism

Act utilitarianism states moral actions are the ones that will produce the most utility in the situation. The value of an action is not determined by law; an action is moral when it benefits the most people. Examples of act utilitarianism are specific actions. Not killing a specific person will prevent sadness for that person's family. Opening the door for the person carrying a box will make that person happy. In some situations, the pain and pleasure are weighed out for the greatest utility in direct calculations. For example five people are shipwrecked with no food. If they kill and eat one person, four people have a chance to survive (happiness), but one will die (pain). If they do not take this action, all five will die (pain). The act that has the greatest utility, then, is for one person to die, because that choice leads to more happiness than pain. There is no consideration given to the act of murder itself as right or wrong. If the greatest utility is served by this murder, then it is right.

Rule utilitarianism states that moral decision-making should abide by a set of rules that will generally tend to maximize utility. Working from the example above concerning the shipwrecked people, a rule utilitarian might not kill choose to kill one to save everyone else, because he/she assumes that if everyone broke the rule "do not kill an innocent person" the consequences would turn out far worse than if all ten people died. To a rule utilitarian, having a law against murder is good because if everyone follows the law, society will be more orderly, because people won't kill each other randomly, and people can be in public and private spaces without fear.

In terms of justice, a rule utilitarian believes the state has a function in meting out punishment, because the law says it is a state function. An act utilitarian may see justice as an individual responsibility; often vigilantes display act utilitarian thinking: "If I kill this serial murderer, more people will be safe." The fact that there is a law against murder may be irrelevant to the utilitarian. Newer versions of utilitarianism have also emerged, including:

1. **Preference utilitarianism** states that as action is best when it satisfied the most preferences, either in themselves or according to their strength of order of importance.
2. **Cost-benefit analysis** states one choice is better than another if it is the least costly compared with the benefits expected.

Ethics: Theory and Practice

Chapter 3 Review Questions

1. Which of the following is not a normative ethical theory?
    a. Act utilitarianism
    b. Rule utilitarianism
    c. Psychological egoism
    d. Contractarianism
2. If stranded on a deserted island with three other people, which ethical theory would you prefer they followed?
    a. Act utilitarianism
    b. Rule utilitarianism
    c. Ethical egoism
    d. Social contract theory
3. What is an important difference between ethical egoism and utilitarianism?
    a. Ethical egoism concerns how people *do* act. Utilitarianism concerns how people *should* act.
    b. Ethical egoism is a normative theory, while utilitarianism is non-normative.
    c. The main tenet of ethical egoism is that people should act in their own self-interest, while utilitarianism maintains we should consider everyone's interests.
    d. Ethical egoism concerns itself with the greatest happiness principle for the most people, whereas utilitarianism maintains that the greatest utility lies in serving the self.
4. When trying to decide how to allocate funds for public projects, most governments depend on_____to help them make decisions.
    a. Rule utilitarianism
    b. Ethical egoism
    c. Cost-benefit analysis
    d. Hedonic calculus
5. Most people agree that the an acceptable limit to liberty is
    a. The Harm Principle
    b. The General Will
    c. Utilitarian Justification
    d. Cost-benefit Analysis

Chapter 4: Deontological Theories

Learning Objectives
After reading this chapter, you should be able to:

1. Identify and explain Kant's three formulations of the categorical imperative.
2. Identify and describe the relationships among Kant's hypothetical imperatives.
3. Describe criticism of deontological theories.
4. Explain why Kantianism is based on rationality.
5. Explain the pluralistic account of William David Ross.

Deontological Ethics

As stated in Chapter 1, deontology is the science of duty. This approach focuses on the rightness or wrongness of motives. It is also described as duty or obligation based ethics, because deontologists believe that ethical rules bind you to your duty. These duties or obligations are usually determined by God; therefore, being moral is often a matter of obeying God. **Divine Command Theory** is an example of deontological theory.

Immanuel Kant

Immanuel Kant (1724-1804) paved a new way for the thought processes of ethics. He did not take the standard role many before him did; instead, he chose to question, as did Socrates, the wrongness of human acts. Humans are able to choose and judge what actions they take for rightness. When one chooses to commit a wrongful act, that person will not be looked upon favorably.

In one of Kant's writings, he described and distinguished between what is good, what is not good, and the factors that determine this. He believed good will is the only good that is without qualification in existence, while explaining how something can only be good if it is compatible with good itself. Kant helped to relate this in regards to one performing a duty out of duty or just doing it for no other purpose. This, in turn, is what makes a good person good. In addition, it is the presence of self-governing reason in each person that Kant thought offered decisive grounds for viewing each individual as possessed of equal worth and deserving of equal respect.

Kantianism is a deontological, act-based, human valuing philosophy. Kant believed people were inherently bad and that we needed to use our reason to come up with a moral framework to transcend mortal life and ultimately gain entrance to heaven. To do this, people have to live by acts that are as selfless as possible.

Kant believed moral principles were objects of rational choice. The central idea of Kant's ethic is the emphasis on the importance of reason and the rational nature of moral principles. He believed that the meaning of morality was *duty*, simply for the sake of duty. Since the only thing that is unconditionally good, without qualification, is good will, he believed we must act from duty to have goodwill. Kant felt that morality could not be confused with self-interest, regardless of how enlightened the interest.

Major tenets of Kant's moral theory include:
1. **Personal autonomy** – People are capable of self-rule. People make their own choices, whereas things cannot choose for themselves. People use things. People should not use other people because it denies their personal autonomy.
2. **Value of intentions (acts)/consequences** – Value lies in intention, not in consequence. If people have the right motives, they have no liability in the outcome because they had the right intent. If their actions render a favorable consequence, they cannot accept credit for the outcome. Therefore, individuals may neither accept praise nor blame for consequences.

Categorical Imperatives

One of Kant's best-known topics is the **Categorical Imperative** (CI). An imperative is a command that tells us to exercise our wills in a particular way. According to Kant, there are two types of imperatives, categorical and hypothetical. **Hypothetical imperatives** are based on individual desires; for example, "if I want to pass the test, I ought to study," is not a moral imperative because it is contingent on a want, and can be avoided by changing the desires. Categorical imperatives, however, are based on rational thought and universal in nature. They are things everyone ought to do, no matter what the conditions. It is the categorical imperative that is a basic principle of Kantianism.

Kant uses the categorical imperative as the ultimate test of morality in any situation. He assumes that every voluntary act is based upon a maxim of one kind or another. A **maxim** is a moral statement or rule of universal truth that the will of an individual uses in making a decision. Kant's search for the supreme principle of morality began with the concept of a categorical imperative that generated the first formula and maxim.

Ethics: Theory and Practice

First Formulation – The Formula of Universal Law and Nature

Maxim: We are never permitted to commit any act that we cannot will as a universal/natural law.

Moral obligations are universal; that is, they are unconditional and apply to everyone. One way to test the morality of any act would be to consider whether you are able to will it for everyone. To will something universally is similar to willing it as law, since law has a degree of universality. Kant observed that all of nature seemed to follow a universal law (e.g., birth, life, death). He saw a harmony in all living things that he felt could be duplicated by human beings. He viewed nature as a system governed by laws. Therefore he thought that we should always ask whether an action is a universal law of nature.

In the first formulation, he discusses how moral reasoning decisions are made. To understand why one makes a decision to act in a certain way, the following considerations must be made: (a) Would said action follow universal law? (b) Is it conceivable? (c) If it is, then would this action then be taken? If so, one can accept this action as morally permissible. Kant also felt that if some standard of the rational of the categorical imperative was violated, then immorality was the end result.

Freedom plays a central role in Kant's ethics. He believed reason and freedom are one and the same, yet theoretical reason and practical freedom have inherent differences. One would not be able to demonstrate freedom while the other would make that assumption, respectively. Kant states we must think of ourselves as free and take the common sense approach. The thought process one has will influence how one then acts.

Kant then considered the motive for following a categorical imperative that led to the creation of the second formula. This formula represents the <u>matter</u> of the moral law, the result of acting from a law valid for all rational beings.

Second Formulation – The Formula of Humanity

Maxim: Always treat people not as a means, but as an end.
First, this formula tells us to respect ourselves and other human beings. Kant called this **respect for persons** and believed it was a principle of humanity. Kant thought that human beings occupy a

special place in creation and other things only have the value that human beings give them. Because we have personal autonomy—we are rational and capable of making our own decisions and guiding our conduct by reason—humans have dignity.

Because of this, humans have the duty of beneficence (doing good) to all persons. We may never manipulate people in order to achieve our purposes.

Second, it tells us to acknowledge the intrinsic value in people rather than the instrumental value. Kant believed that people are precious creations of God; therefore, they may not be used as instruments for attaining one's own desires. Each individual must be treated in a way that recognizes his or her uniqueness and value. The second CI, which is dictated by reasoning for moral action, states that one is never to use another as a means to an end. This is important to understanding Kant's moral theory, as a whole, in that humans are a means unto themselves.

The third formula draws on ideas expressed in the previous formulas.

Third Formulation

The Formula of Autonomy

Maxim: The decision to act according to a maxim is regarded as having made the maxim a universal law.

When we make a Kantian moral decision, we act freely. An external source does not decide for us. The Formula of Autonomy makes explicit the value and dignity of humanity. It focuses on our being potential authors of laws valid for all rational beings. It is our status as potential authors of universal law that is the basis of our dignity.

The Formula of the Kingdom of Ends

Maxim: We ought to act only by maxims that would harmonize with a possible kingdom of ends.

Kant defined a kingdom as various rational beings systematically united through common laws. Rational beings constitute a kingdom to the extent that their ends constitute a system. To constitute a system not only must their ends be mutually compatible, but they must be mutually reinforcing as well, constituting a system of shared ends. Universal adherence to the laws of a kingdom of ends would result in furthering the ends of all rational beings in a single teleological system.

These three formulas represent the same principle and differ only in representing different aspects of that same principle. Kant claimed that for appraisal of an action the first formula is best, but ideally all three should be applied.

John Rawls

John Rawls was a 20th century philosopher who attempted to associate Kantian philosophy with the law. Unlike Kant, he was concerned with the issue of fairness and social justice. He developed a **social contract** theory of justice. To review, social contract describes a broad class of theories that try to explain the ways in which people form states and/or maintain social order.

Rawls develops the idea that justice is fairness in his classic book, *A Theory of Justice* (1971). In this text, Rawls says the rational individual would only choose to establish a society that would at least conform to the following two rules:

1. **The Liberty Principle**: Each person is to have an equal right to the most extensive basic liberty compatible with a similar liberty for others. This rule requires basic and universal respect for persons as a minimum standard for all just institutions. In reality, there are significant differences between individuals that, under conditions of liberty, will lead to social and economic inequalities, despite moral equality.
2. **The Difference Principle**: Social and economic inequalities are to be arranged so that (a) they are to be of the greatest benefit of the least-advantaged members of society, consistent with the just savings principle (the difference principle); and (b) offices and positions must be open to everyone under conditions of fair equality of opportunity.

This rule suggests that it will be to the advantage to all (similar to the utility principle). The idea of *fair equality of opportunity* means not only that offices and positions are distributed on the basis of merit, but that everyone, regardless of socio-economic position, has a reasonable opportunity to develop the skills which are assessed to determine merit.

Rawls argued that the two principles would be used by representative parties in the **original position**, a utopic state where everything was fair and equitable. In this state, it would appear easy for parties to decide what was or was not fair and just. To prevent each party from making choices that benefitted only themselves, Rawls devised the **veil of ignorance** that deprived them of information about particular characteristics such as age, race, wealth, and natural abilities, as discussed in Chapter 3.

William David Ross

William David Ross, a 20th century philosopher, has been said to hold a position that is representative of **pluralistic deontology**. His theories reflect **moral realism** and **intuitionism**. While mostly deontological, Ross's theory is somewhat in between stricter deontological theories, like Kant's, and teleological theories like utilitarianism. This means that he held there are several distinct moral considerations that bear on the rightness of an action. Ross argued that utilitarianism was an inadequate moral theory because it failed to appropriately account for primary moral concerns of interpersonal relationships. He saw problems with Kant's absolute rules, which had the potential to result in conflicting obligations. Ross thought that when obligations conflict we should look for the greatest balance of right over wrong.

According to Ross, there are several prima facie, or conditional, duties that we can use to determine what we ought to do. A **prima facie duty** is a duty that is obligatory, unless it is overridden by another duty. In other words, where there is a prima facie duty to do something, there is at least a fairly strong presumption in favor of doing it.

Ross's prima facie duties include:
1. **Duty of beneficence** – A duty to help other people increase pleasure and improve character.
2. **Duty of non-malfeasance** – A duty to avoid harming other people.
3. **Duty of justice** – A duty to ensure people get what they deserve.
4. **Duty of self-improvement** – A duty to improve ourselves.
5. **Duty of reparation** – A duty to recompense someone if you have acted wrongly towards him/her.
6. **Duty of gratitude** – A duty to benefit people who have benefited us.
7. **Duty of promise-keeping** – A duty to act according to explicit and implicit promises, including the implicit promise to tell the truth.

Each of these duties needs to be taken into consideration when deciding which duty should be acted upon. When more than one of these duties applies to a person in a situation, only one should be acted upon. Ross does not provide a principle upon which to determine what our actual duty is in any circumstance. However, he does seem to show preference to non-malfeasance over beneficence.

Unlike prima facie duties, our **actual** or **concrete duty** is the duty we should perform in the particular situation of choice. Whatever one's **actual duty** is, one is morally bound to perform it. A prima facie duty is fundamentally different from a concrete or actual duty. It is more of a moral reason. Since one prima facie duty can outweigh another in a particular situation, the prima facie (which means "appears to be at first glance") duty cannot be an obligation that must be performed in any circumstance. By actual duty, Ross means what we have been referring to as a moral obligation. Ross has been criticized for his terminology.

Ethics: Theory and Practice

Chapter 4 Review Questions

1. Kant's Second Formulation (the Formula of Humanity) can be used to justify
    a. Abolishing human trafficking.
    b. Campaigning for women's rights.
    c. Establishing laws against rape.
    d. All of the above.
2. According to Kantianism, we have personal autonomy because we
    a. Have a duty to be responsible for others.
    b. Have the ability to make our own decisions based on reason.
    c. Use maxims to guide our own decision making.
    d. Use people for our own ends.
3. A scholarship panel which looks at applications that have been stripped of identifying content (e.g., names, ages, addresses, schools) can be said to be operating using
    a. The Formula of Humanity.
    b. The Original Position.
    c. The Hypothetical Imperative.
    d. The Veil of Ignorance.
4. A tax formula that has lower-income people paying a smaller percentage in tax than higher-income people could be said to be operating under
    a. The Original Position.
    b. The Difference Principle.
    c. The Liberty Principle.
    d. The Social Contract.
5. A doctor treating a patient with a complicated heart condition is faced with two options. The first option is an experimental surgery that could cure the condition quickly, but the procedure comes with considerable risk of injury and death. The other option is a proven treatment course of medications, but this course takes more than two years, and the medications can have significant side effects. The prima facie duties the doctor is weighing are:
    a. The duty of justice and the duty of reparations
    b. The duty of beneficence and the duty of non-malfeasance
    c. The duty of gratitude and the duty of promise-keeping
    d. The duty of non-malfeasance and the duty of justice

Chapter 5: Virtue Ethics, Natural Law Theory, Communitarianism, and Feminine Ethics

Learning Objectives
After reading this chapter, you should be able to:

1. Distinguish between moral and non-moral values.
2. Describe the conflict between the ethics of being and the ethics of doing.
3. Explain Aristotle's idea of what constitutes a good person.
4. Define Plato's concepts of the soul and the virtuous person.
5. Understand the development of Natural Law theory throughout history to the present- day understanding of human rights.
6. Explain the importance of virtue in Hume's theory.
7. Describe why the ethics of care is thought to be a feminine ethic.
8. Explain why Hume thought that reason is and ought to be a slave of the passions.

Virtue Ethics

In order to identify human virtues, one needs to have a firm grasp on what the human purpose is. Throughout time, inconsistency in defining these virtues has been the norm. Homer, Aristotle, Thomas Aquinas, and Benjamin Franklin all created lists of human virtues, many of which fail to overlap the others. The first systematic description of virtue ethics was recorded by Aristotle in his famous work, **The Nicomachean Ethics.** It expands on the understanding of ethics due to its heavy dependency on the concept of virtue. According to Aristotle, when people are better able to regulate their emotions and their reason, they acquire good habits of **character**. This, in turn, helps us reach morally correct decisions when we are faced with difficult choices.

Aristotle closely observed nature. He believed nature was purposive and did nothing in vain. The purpose is what Aristotle called *telos*, the Greek word for goal. **Natural Law** is considered teleological because of its emphasis on a goal embedded in the nature of things.

According to Aristotle, if morality refers to our actions, and our actions are a reflection of our beliefs, then morality ought to address what we believe.

Ethics: Theory and Practice

When discuss moral life we should define the ideals necessary for justice and morality. Then we should try to develop those ideals in ourselves and in our society. Unlike Plato, Aristotle focused on the idea of a potentially perfect society.

Soul

The Platonic soul is made up of three parts: the **logos** (mind), **thymos** (emotion), and **eros** (desire). Each part has a specific, defined function in a balanced and peaceful soul. Following the ideas of his teacher Socrates, Plato considered the soul as the essence of people, and responsible for deciding how we behave. Plato considered the soul to be an eternal occupant of our being that is continually reborn in subsequent bodies after our death.

Aristotle, following Plato, defined the soul as the core or essence of a living being. He also argued against the soul having a completely separate existence. In Aristotle's view, a living thing's soul is its own activity. Plato saw the soul as a ghostly occupant of the body. In Aristotle's view, the soul is part of a living body and, therefore, cannot be immortal.

Although the soul is not a tangible object, it is not separable from the body in Aristotle's view. By his account, the soul has three components: our **passion**, our **faculties**, and our states of **character**. Based on these components, his notion of the soul parallels our current notion of the mind.

Aristotle defines supreme good as an activity of the rational soul in accordance with virtue.

Virtue

Virtue can be translated as excellence and described as harmony of the soul's parts. Aristotle thought of virtues as states of character. According to Aristotle, there are two basic types of virtues: moral and intellectual.

Moral virtues describe feeling, choosing, and acting well. There are eight moral virtues: **prudence, justice, fortitude, courage, liberality, magnificence, magnanimity,** and **temperance**. Moral virtues are acquired by habit and must be cultivated. They are acquired with effort and developed through practice. Aristotle also describes non-moral virtues as being anything less than the human ideal. These are normative values about which traits are worthy of esteem.

Intellectual virtues are described as a kind of wisdom acquired by teaching. Aristotle identified nine intellectual virtues and divided them into three types: **theoretical, practical,** and **productive**. The most important intellectual virtues were types of wisdom: **sophia** (theoretical wisdom) and **phronesis** (practical wisdom).

Aristotle said one should strive to become a virtuous person. A virtuous person is a morally good person, and therefore virtues are good traits. The premise of virtue ethics lies in the belief that in order to live a moral life one must begin by developing good character. A follower of virtue ethics would argue that morality is not about "What should I do?" but rather, "What should I be?"

The Mean

Aristotle argued that each of the moral virtues was a mean between two corresponding vices. Virtue is a balance point between a deficiency and an excess of a trait. It consists of finding an appropriate middle ground between two extremes; therefore, each virtue has not one opposite, but two. The point of greatest virtue lies not in the exact middle, but at a **golden mean**, which is sometimes closer to one extreme than the other.

Morals

Virtue ethics further our understanding of morality because of the emphasis they place on the role played by motives in responding to moral question. To have virtues guiding our actions is to have some particular motivation initiating the act. This means that certain virtues are a necessity for correct moral decisions. In other words, correct moral decisions require correct motives. While other moral theories share a difficulty in dealing with complicated moral calculations over what action should be taken or which moral duty should be acted upon, virtue theories remove the difficulty. The premise of virtue theories is that once one is successful in becoming the person one wants to be, making correct moral decisions will simply come naturally.

Eudemonia

Eudemonia is usually translated from Greek as happiness or well-being, and in the context of virtue ethics, "human flourishing," but it has some of the same connotations as "success," since in addition to living well it includes doing well. In this sense, eudemonia is an objective state rather than a subjective one. Aristotle refers to happiness as an activity, which distinguishes his conception of happiness both from our modern conception of the word and from virtue, which Aristotle calls a disposition. We tend to think of happiness as an emotional state. Therefore, we define happiness as something we <u>are</u>, rather than something we <u>do</u>. To Aristotle, happiness characterizes a well-lived life, regardless of the emotional state of the person experiencing it.

Ethics: Theory and Practice

In the Western philosophical tradition, Aristotle states, the most conspicuous illustration of eudemonia is the proper goal of human life. Exercising the human quality of reason is the soul's most nourishing activity. Like Plato before him, Aristotle argued that pursuing eudemonia was an activity only achievable in the human community. Aristotle believed that virtue is necessary for happiness, while Plato said virtue is enough for happiness.

Although eudemonia was first popularized by Aristotle, it now generally belongs to the tradition of virtue theories. For the virtue theorist, eudemonia describes that state achieved by the person who lives the proper human life. This is an outcome that can be reached by practicing the virtues. A virtue is a habit or quality that allows the bearer to succeed at his, her, or its purpose.

Natural Law

When people talk about human rights, they mean rights that they believe that all human beings, regardless of the rules of their respective societies or governments, are entitled to enjoy. These rights are to those things that are essential for functioning well as a human being. According to the **1948 United Nations Declaration of Human Rights**, general welfare needs, including food, clothing, shelter, and security are basic human rights. These things are necessary to allow human beings to function well. We also have the phrase "crimes against humanity" which was used to prosecute Nazi war criminals at Nuremburg. This concept assumes a moral law that supersedes any law of any government. Most people will agree that there are certain things people should not do to other people, such as murder. But as we delve into this topic we shall see that not everyone agrees about what basic human rights are.

The idea of human rights is rooted in the theory of **Natural Law**. Aristotle formulated the theory of Natural Law through observing order in nature. Natural Law is therefore considered a **teleological** view. Aristotle observed that nature always followed the same path. An acorn always grew into an oak, instead of a pine or an elm. A tadpole always grew into a frog instead of a cow or a bird. The end goal or purpose of the process is to be the best oak or frog it can be. This is its **good**. Aristotle posited "the good is that at which all things aim." The good of the musician is to make music. The good of the shipbuilder is to build ships. The good of a human being, therefore, is perfecting the characteristics specific to being human. That which makes humans unique from seeds and animals is a **rational element** that allows humans to know the world and the truth, and to guide choice and action.

Ethics: Theory and Practice

Aristotle recognized that humans could choose to do what is their good or act against it. He theorized that when humans use their rational element to perfect their capacities and abilities, they function well and are therefore happy. Following this line of reasoning, the ultimate good of humans is happiness, prosperity, and blessedness—or **eudemonia**.

The Romans, in tackling the challenges of governing a multinational, multicultural, pluralistic commonwealth encompassing many nationalities, religions, ethnicities, and legal systems, needed a code of laws that would be uniformly enforced upon all of their subjects regardless of race, color, or religious creed. Of the common legal core that made up the Roman code, **Cicero** (106-43 B.C.E.) wrote in his *De republica*, "True law is right reason in agreement with nature; it is of universal application, unchanging and everlasting; it summons to duty by its commands, and adverts from wrongdoing by its prohibitions...We cannot be freed from its obligations by Senate or People, and we need not look outside ourselves for an expounder or interpreter of it...." This common legal core could be found in the commonalities that existed in the codes of various peoples—a *jus gentium*. Medieval theologian **Thomas Aquinas** (1224-1274 C.E.) combined Aristotle's theory of Natural Law and Roman *jus gentium* with Christian theology to posit that Natural Law reflects a **divine law**, a plan for the universe, whose author is God. According to Aquinas, the order found in nature and in human nature is created by God and reflects God's will. Therefore, moral good is found through following the innate tendencies of human nature. Moral good is defined through the rational element: treating ourselves and others as being capable of understanding and of having free choice is good. Those things that help us pursue truth (education, freedom of expression) and enable us to choose freely (self-discipline, options, reflection) are morally good. Those things that hinder pursuit of truth (deceit, lack of information) and our ability to choose (coercion, limited options) are morally bad. Furthermore, Aquinas observed that humans are social creatures that function best when they cooperate.

Two important principles of the Natural Law theory serve to tie together the nature of human beings and moral law. The **Principle of Forfeiture** serves to resolve conflicts in basic values. It states that if one threatens another, then the one imposing the harm no longer has rights. The **Principle of Double Effect** deals with doing something morally permissible for the purpose of achieving some good while knowing that it also may have a bad secondary effect. Certain conditions must be met, however, for this to be right. First, the act must be morally permissible. One cannot do what is wrong to bring about a good end. Second, the person who acts must intend to bring about the good end rather than the harmful result. Third, the good results must outweigh the bad ones. The idea that no man is an island and everyone has a role to play as they perfect their rational element was a founding principal of the Enlightenment, which led to the waning of the power of monarchs and despots and the eventual formation of the United States and other modern governments.

The works of **John Locke** (1632-1704 C.E.) had a great impact on the leading voices of the Enlightenment. Moving forward from Aristotle and Aquinas, John Locke proposed because of Natural Law that every human being had the **natural right** to life, liberty, and property. These words were echoed later in the Declaration of Independence of the United States as "life, liberty, and the pursuit of happiness." The ideas are built into the United States Constitution and society (freedom of speech, free public education, freedom of information, etc.) and interpretations of these ideas form the basis for various political ideologies.

Criticisms of Natural Law Theory

It is these differing interpretations that highlight the questions about the Natural Law theory. There is disagreement among philosophers regarding the essence of human nature. There are those who posit that humans are by nature deceitful, selfish, and evil. Other critics make the point that just because something exists in nature, it is not automatically good (i.e. disease, drought, flood, etc.) Additionally, the theory can be used to support widely divergent concepts at the same time. For example, it has been used to support capitalism, socialism, and libertarianism.

Furthermore, as the law is based on observation of nature, the theory of evolution, which is based on mutation and survival of the fittest, makes end goals (the good) arbitrary.

Communitarianism

Philosophers have identified two features of human nature that seem to make human beings unique: their rationality and their sociality. Human beings do not merely live in groups like some other animals. Rather, they understand themselves in light of the identities they share as members of groups and the attachments they have with the people around them. This human characteristic led to a position in moral philosophy called **communitarianism**, which holds that morality is constituted by the ideals that define and hold together human groups.

Communitarian ethics is based on the position that everything fundamental in ethics is derived from communal values, traditional practices, social goals, and cooperative virtues. Communitarians believe in the idea of a "common good." Communitarians look at shared values, ideals, and goals of a community, rather than focus on a collective individual welfare (as in utilitarianism). They believe that even people with very different values will also have shared values. The important truth in communitarianism is that we are not separate brings, but linked to our community.

Communitarians reject the idea of timeless universal ethical truths based on reason. They believe that moral thinking has, at its core, historical traditions of communities.

Communitarianism accepts the standards of existing groups as the norm rather than inherently specifying proper moral standards on its own. This is a problematic approach as it forms morality to the pre-endorsed standards of a people, which are often considered patently immoral themselves. For this reason, many philosophers who originally endorsed the communitarianism theme realized that communities, once deemed to align with moral standards, then seemed oppressive (for example, traditional religious communities have held sexist views in that they have endorsed the theory that women are meant to obey and serve men.)

By drawing a parallel with virtue ethics, communitarianism points to where morality <u>should</u> be found as opposed to what it actually consists of. It leaves us void of distinguishing moral standards against which a community can be measured.

David Hume

Many regard **David Hume** as a political **conservative**, sometimes calling him the first conservative philosopher. This is not entirely accurate, if the term conservative is understood in any modern sense. His thoughts contained elements that are, in modern terms, both conservative and liberal, as well as ones that were both contractarian and utilitarian. Hume's conservatism bases moral and social order on human nature and common life rather than supernatural forces.

David Hume's views on human action and motivation defined the cornerstone of his ethical theory. He conceived moral or ethical sentiments to be either intrinsically motivating or the providers of reasons for action. Considering that one cannot be motivated by reason alone and that passions were requisite, Hume argued that reason cannot be behind morality.

The **is-ought problem**, (also known as **Hume's guillotine**) was articulated by Hume, who noted that many writers define what <u>ought to be</u>, on the foundation of statements surrounding <u>what is</u>. There seems to be a significant difference between descriptive statements (about <u>what is</u>) and prescriptive statements (about what <u>ought to be</u>). Hume is famous for his position that we cannot derive *ought* from *is*. This is the view that statements of moral obligation cannot simply be deduced from statements of fact. For many, Hume's question is unanswerable. However, there are a few arguments that have been proposed that claim to show that an *ought* can actually be derived from an *is*. One such argument was designed by **John Searle.** His argument tried to show that the act of making a promise, by definition, places one under an obligation, and that any such obligation is equivalent to an *ought*.

For Hume, following the rules of the moral community is an essential aspect of morality. Hume thought that what motivates us to action is passion, not reason. Hume's theory says that an act is good only if it is done from a virtuous motive--a motive, that is, that would be approved by an impartial observer.

Hume concludes that there are four irreducible categories of **qualities** that exhaustively constitute moral virtue:

1. Qualities useful to others, such as benevolence, meekness, charity, justice, fidelity, and veracity.
2. Qualities useful to oneself, such as industry, perseverance, and patience.
3. Qualities immediately agreeable to others, such as wit, eloquence, and cleanliness.
4. Qualities immediately agreeable to oneself, such as good humor, self-esteem, and pride.

For Hume, most morally significant actions are ones that fall into more than one of these categories.

Hume's position in ethics, which is based on his empiricist theory of the mind, is best known for asserting four theses:

1. Reason alone cannot be a motive to the will, but rather is the "slave

of the passions."
2. Morals are not derived from reason.
3. Morals are derived from the moral sentiments: feelings of approval and disapproval felt by spectators who contemplate a character trait or action.
4. While some virtue and vices are natural, others, such as justice, are artificial.

There is much debate about what Hume intends by each of these theses and how he argues for them. They are best understood in the context of Hume's meta-ethical theory and his ethic of virtue and vice.

In the first thesis Hume said that reason is and ought to be a slave of the passions. By this, Hume means that reason's role in guiding actions is limited to its utility in aiding the fulfillment of desire in responding to the passions of the self. Hume means that arguments alone do not move people; one must have an emotional pull toward actualizing the results of one's reasoning. For Hume, the ultimate basis of morality was the act of feeling. We act on our moral positions because we are born with a psychological predisposition toward empathy with other persons because we are made uncomfortable by their suffering. Hume thought that we have a natural inclination to be moral in situations were being moral conflicts with self-interest.

Feminine Ethics

The **ethics of care** is a normative ethical theory that was developed by feminists in the second half of the twentieth century during the women's movement.

While consequentialist and deontological ethical theories emphasize universal standards and impartiality, ethics of care is a **communitarian** approach that emphasizes the importance of relationships.

The basis of the theory is the recognition of:
1. The interdependence of all individuals for achieving their interests.
2. This belief that those particularly vulnerable to our choices and their outcomes deserve extra consideration, to be measured according to:

   a) Their level of vulnerability to one's choices.
   b) Their level of affectedness by one's choices and no one else's.
   The necessity of attending to the contextual details of the situation

in order to protect and promote the actual specific interests of those involved.

While some feminists have criticized care-based ethics for reinforcing traditional female stereotypes, others have embraced part of this paradigm under the theoretical concept of care-focused feminism.

Carol Gilligan, a psychologist who studied the differences in morality between the sexes, found that men tended to define morality in more global terms, and women used more affective terms. Her body of work, and others, led to the notion of a female moral perspective. This perspective focuses on the context of relationships, emphasizes responsiveness and responsibility to others, and focuses on love, trust, and human bonding.

When questioning men and women about the need for morality, women stressed the need to protect individuals from harm and the trauma that might result from that harm. Women are able to empathize with others and tend to focus on feelings associated with real-life situations. The context of women's moral decision making is said to be one of relatedness to harm that might befall others. Women are able to empathize with others and are concerned about how they might feel if the same thing happened to them. Caring and compassion are key virtues. The primary obligation is not to turn away from others in need.

Ethics of care is also a basis for care-focused feminists theorizing on maternal ethics. Feminist theorists suggest caring should be performed and care givers valued in both public and private spheres. This proposed paradigm shift in ethics encourages that an ethic of caring be the social responsibility of both men and women.

Ethics of care theories are similar to Hume's notion of **sympathy**. According to Hume, sympathy is the natural tendency of people to share feelings with others. He believed sympathy was a natural part of human psychology to have a social nature and sympathetic identification with others.

Hume's sympathy is the means of communication through which we come to understand the sentiments (pains and pleasures) of others and from which we can determine vice and virtue. Sympathy is seen as the tool to help us bridge the gap between the self and others. Both theories find that his is limited to a person's immediate social network, not necessarily extended to people in general.

Ethics: Theory and Practice

Chapter 5 Review Questions

1. The virtuous mean between cowardice and recklessness is
    a. Honor.
    b. Patience.
    c. Courage.
    d. Temperance.
2. Implied in the phrase "crimes against humanity" is the assumption that
    a. There are universal rights common to all human beings.
    b. Human beings are inherently criminal.
    c. All governments have the same laws.
    d. The soul will be punished for crime.
3. Which of the following would Thomas Aquinas oppose?
    a. Public education
    b. Censorship
    c. Marriage
    d. Free choice
4. How does understanding the term *eudemonia* impact our understanding of the Declaration of Independence?
    a. It helps to define the "pursuit of happiness" as the striving for success, contentment, and the ultimate human good.
    b. It helps to explain why the signers of the Declaration felt it necessary to declare their independence.
    c. It helps to clarify the meaning of independence.
    d. It helps to understand Locke's influence on the formation of the government.
5. Which of these government agencies is most likely to reflect the ethics of care?
    a. Department of Justice
    b. Department of Energy
    c. Department of Health and Human Services
    d. Department of Homeland Security

Chapter 6: Existentialism and Nietzsche

Learning Objectives
After reading this chapter, you should be able to:

1. Distinguish between the two types of freedom identified by Simone de Beauvoir.
2. Understand how existentialists believe values are created.
3. Compare and contrast Simone de Beauvoir's and Nietzsche's philosophies.
4. Distinguish between master and slave morality.

Existentialism

Existentialism is a philosophy that focuses on finding one's self and the meaning of life through free will, choice, and personal responsibility. Existentialists believe that people are continually searching to discover whom and what they are in life as they exercise choices based on their experiences, beliefs, and outlooks. Personal choices are unique and independent of an objective form of truth. An existentialist believes that a person should be required to choose and be responsible without the help of laws, ethnic rules, or traditions. Because existentialist ethics reject the idea of absolute moral laws and most religion-based ethics, they have to find moral significance without these traditional justifications.

There are a wide variety of philosophical, religious, and political ideologies that comprise existentialism, so there can be no universal agreement in an arbitrary set of ideals and beliefs. Each ideology simply seeks the most individual freedom for people within a society.

Nietzsche: On the Genealogy of Morals

Friedrich Nietzsche (1844-1900) wrote *On the Genealogy of Morals*, which is made up of three essays. In each, **Nietzsche** uses a genealogical method to examine the origins and meanings of our different moral concepts and questions, and critiques the value of our moral judgments.
Nietzsche's main undertaking is to question the value of our morality. Nietzsche characterized his era as nihilistic, because of its unwavering faith in a science that describes the world as meaningless and under the influence of unchanging laws. **Nihilism** is the literal belief in nothing.

Ethics: Theory and Practice

The first essay: Good and Evil, Good and Bad

This essay begins with an explanation of how the terms *good* and *bad* got their meaning: Originally, there were two kinds of individuals, the noble, powerful, superior, and high-minded, and the lower class, low-minded and common.

Nietzsche thought that the common people resented the power of the ruling nobility, causing them to develop an alternate set of values in rebellion. These values, such as altruism, peace, equality, and humility became associated with the powerless and the poor.

This contrast describes what Nietzsche calls **master morality** and **slave morality**. Nietzsche details and compares the origins of the values he associates with nobility and the values associated with slaves. He claims that the word *good* refers to the noble ruling class because they had the power to define what was good. Common people (slaves) were thought to be too simple minded to make these judgments.

Hatred and the desire for others to conform are essential features of the slave morality. The noble may at times hate, but it is not essential to his/her character to do so, and part of the reason for this is psychological. When a powerful person hates they discharge this through direct action. The weak cannot do this; they must contain their hatred, which acts as a psychological toxin, poisoning the spirit. This is the cause of **rancor and resentment**. Nietzsche calls the noble person's feeling of being superior as the **pathos of distance**. He believes that it is through the pathos of distance that *good* and *bad* first acquired their meaning. That is, *good* was defined as those who were superior, noble, and privileged; while *bad* was associated with those who were common and low.

The second essay: Guilt, Bad Conscience, and the Like

Here Nietzsche traces the origins of concepts such as guilt and **punishment**. He claims that they were not originally based on any sense of moral violation. Guilt was a result of a debt that was owed, and punishment was a form of repayment. Nietzsche believed that the rise of slave morality brought about the present meanings of these terms. He believed that societies' slave morality caused humans to see themselves as sinners and inhibit their animal instincts for aggression and cruelty. These instincts were instead turned inward by use of **sublimation**, the act of repressing one's immediate instincts for power in order to achieve a less harmful expression of power.

The third essay: What is the Meaning of Ascetic Ideals?
The third essay opposes **asceticism**, the practice of the denial of psychological or physical desires to attain a spiritual ideal. Nietzsche sees asceticism as the expression of a weak or flawed will, and an attempt to subdue animal instincts. He explains that man would rather will nothing, than not will at all.

Morality is generally treated as sacred because we assume that there is some transcendental ground for our morals, such as religion, reason, or tradition. Nietzsche's genealogical method challenges our assumption that *good* and *bad* have always held the same meanings. He shows how these terms have evolved, demonstrating a lack of continuity or absolute truth of our present moral concepts.

Therefore, Nietzsche claims that in order to remain free and gain our own perspective we should not allow ourselves to be dominated by a particular will. We should not give in to one particular meaning or interpretation of a thing. A will should reject absolutes and consider matters from many different perspectives. This doctrine, which has deeply influenced post-modern thought, is called **perspectivism**.

Because they can have different, even conflicting, meanings over the course of their existence, Nietzsche does not believe that concepts are based in reality. Instead he explores what influences the different meanings that concepts have adopted over time. He concludes by finding force and will. All of existence, Nietzsche asserts, is a struggle between different wills for the feeling of power. He describes this **will to power** as a constant competition with others, often for no other purpose than to feel superior to those who have been overcome. He argues that our current ascetic morality comes from a resentment and hatred toward anything that is more powerful, stronger, or healthier than ourselves.

To Nietzsche nothing is sacred, absolute, or even true. Our

morality is not a set of duties passed down from God, but an arbitrary code that has randomly evolved. The only conviction he holds is that everything and everyone is in a constant battle for more power. The only virtue is a will that is powerful, and free from bad conscience, hatred, and resentment. He sees our present ascetic morality as being harmful to the health and prosperity of our species.

Simone de Beauvoir

Simone de Beauvoir was a French philosopher who, with Sartre, was a leading exponent of existentialist philosophy. Her most famous work, *The Second Sex*, marked the beginning of modern feminism.

Simone de Beauvoir also authored *The Ethics of Ambiguity*, where she defines two types of freedom: **creative freedom** and **free will**. Free will represents one's inescapable ability to make choices about his or her actions. Whether or not to use creative freedom is a choice. Not choosing creative freedom would rob a person of his or her unique, true, and meaningful life.

Existentialists such as de Beauvoir value freedom above all else. Freedom means that you will not blindly accept the values handed down to you in childhood. It involves deciding your own values through the course of living and being an **authentic** being.

De Beauvoir describes the widespread attitude of bad faith and attributes it to the person she identifies as the **serious** individual. **Bad faith** can be described as living in self-deception and involves three types of conduct.

First, bad faith involves a shift between the two definitions of the French verb *être*, which means "to be." The two meanings of "to be" in existentialism are: **being-in-itself**, which is pure being, nothing more than existence, and **being-for-itself**, which is characterized by consciousness or knowledge of existing. The term *bad faith* is a metaphysical pun. It uses both literal definitions of the word *being* to achieve an end that is advantageous, in that it encourages or reinforces existing restraint on one's freedom. One example of this is evident in de Beauvoir's *The Second Sex*, where she writes of the occurrence of life slipping by in an infantile world. This fading of life is due to individuals having been kept in a state of ignorance and servitude, which they don't have the capacity to overcome. Similar to a child, these individuals can only exercise the freedom that is constrained by the universe around them—one that was set up by others before them. We see this example illustrated by slaves who have not obtained the consciousness of their slavery and simply live life as tough there were no alternative.

The second category of bad faith conduct establishes a pursuit of sincerity that is actually insincere in its nature. Sincerity is defined as the determination to be for oneself and for others what one actually is. De Beauvoir believed that if a person never becomes the essential, it is because he/she has failed to bring about this change. Therefore, insincerity is denying one's self and it establishes a foundational excuse for the continuation of living in bad faith.

Finally, bad faith includes as inauthentic attitude toward faith itself. The individual living with bad faith makes no distinction between beliefs. It is just as acceptable to believe the irrational as the rational for this person. With bad faith, the individual moves from the position that all beliefs are equally certain to the perspective that an individual belief is absolutely concrete.

Ethics: Theory and Practice

Chapter 6 Review Questions

1. As a theory, existentialism most resembles which other moral philosophy?
   a. Utilitarianism
   b. Moral relativism
   c. Kantianism
   d. Virtue ethics

2. The word *villain* comes from the word *vilein,* which in the Middle Ages meant "farm servant." The fact that the word now means a "wicked or cruel person" is evidence that supports the theory of
   a. Master and slave morality
   b. Existentialism
   c. Nihilism
   d. Bad faith

3. Nietzsche's perspectivism asserts that in order to remain free and gain our own perspective we should not allow ourselves to be dominated by a particular will. This is doctrine is similar to which other concept?
   a. Rousseau's social contract
   b. Hume's communitarianism
   c. Rawl's liberty principle
   d. Kant's personal autonomy

4. Bad faith can be avoided by
   a. Living authentically.
   b. Living seriously.
   c. Living religiously.
   d. Living obediently.

5. According to de Beauvoir, in childhood, we are necessarily constrained by rules set up by others (e.g., parents, teachers) because we are not ready to take on the responsibility of freedom. As adults, if we continue to submit to the authority of others instead of taking on the responsibility of our own freedom, we are
   a. Being authentic.
   b. Guilty of bad faith.
   c. Using creative freedom.
   d. All of the above.

Ethics: Theory and Practice

Chapter 7: Justice, Rights, and Liberty

Learning Objectives
After reading this chapter, you should be able to:

1. Compare and contrast various principles of justice.
2. Explain the correlativity thesis.
3. Describe types of rights and their relationship to obligations.
4. Explain the conditions required for autonomy.
5. Describe the principles that can justifiably limit liberty.

Justice

The foundations of justice are based on the ideas of social stability, equal dignity, and interdependence. Ethicist **John Rawls** felt the stability of a society depended upon the extent to which the members of that society feel they are being treated justly. If some of a society's members come to feel they are subject to unequal treatment, there will be social unrest. Rawls held that the members of a community depend on each other, and they will remain intact only to the extent that their institutions are just. Immanuel Kant, and others, asserted that human beings are all equal in this respect. All humans have the same dignity, and by virtue of this dignity, they deserve to be equal. Human dignity is violated when individuals are treated unequally on the basis of arbitrary or irrelevant characteristics.

Justice is a pivotal part of ethics and key to moral decision-making. In evaluating any moral decision, we must ask whether our actions treat all persons equally. When conflicts arise, society needs principles of justice that we can all accept as reasonable and fair standards for determining what people deserve. However, saying that justice is giving each person what he or she deserves is not enough. To determine what people deserve, guiding principles have been created.

The **formal principle of justice** treat equals equally and unequals unequally. This is the most fundamental principle of justice and has been widely accepted since it was first defined by Aristotle more than two thousand years ago. **Universalizability** describes the idea that actions should be judged similarly, unless they have morally relevant differences.

Types of Justice

Distributive justice is concerned with society functioning effectively, engaging in efficient and effective production, keeping its members, and sustaining their well-being. Equal distribution is thought to give people a sense of true membership. It also creates the motivation to produce and to be rewarded for one's productivity. Distribution according to need also ensures that everyone's basic needs are met.

Just distribution can be determined by the rules followed in determining a distribution, or by the final outcome. A fair procedure might result in an unfair distribution, or a fair outcome could result from unjust procedures.

In *A Theory of Justice*, **John Rawls** stated that luck determines one's birthplace, social status, and family influences and should not unduly influence the amount of benefits we receive in life. He felt that the goal of distributive justice is to limit the influence of luck so that goods might be distributed in a way that is equally fair and to everyone's advantage.

As explained in chapter four, Rawls had two main principles of justice: The **Liberty Principle** and the **Difference Principle**, which also contains the **Fair Opportunity Principle**. Rawls believed that his two principles would promote **impartiality**, meaning that special privilege would not be given to any party. He found the lack of impartiality a flaw in utilitarianism, claiming that utilitarians mistook impersonality for impartiality.

For others, distributive justice must be a matter of both process and outcome. They believe that in order for people to feel that they have received a fair outcome, the processes of distribution must be fair. In this way, distributive justice is related to concerns about procedural justice.

Retributive justice is founded in the notions of **merit** and **desert**, the idea that people should receive what they deserve. This means that people who work hard deserve the rewards, while those who break the rules deserve to be punished. In addition, people deserve to be treated in the same way they choose to treat others. Wrongdoing is seen as a loss of benefits to someone who was entitled to them, and a gain of benefits to someone who is undeserving. The wrongdoer owes a debt to fellow citizens that will be repaid with punishment.

Retributive justice is in this way backward-looking. Punishment acts to reinforce rules that have been broken, balance the scales of justice, and restore both victim and offender to their appropriate positions relative to each other.

Procedural justice is concerned with making and implementing decisions according to fair processes, because fair procedures are the best guarantee for fair outcomes. People are more willing to accept outcomes they do not like if they feel the procedures used were respectful and dignified.

Procedures are deemed fair if:
1. There is an emphasis on consistency. Fair procedures should guarantee that like cases are treated alike.
2. Those carrying out the procedures are impartial and neutral. Those directly affected by the decisions should have a voice and representation in the process. This is especially important for weaker parties whose voices often go unheard.
3. The processes that are implemented are transparent. Decisions should be reached through open procedures, without secrecy or deception.

The theory of procedural justice is controversial, with a variety of views about what makes a procedure fair. These views tend to fall into three main categories:
1. The outcomes model regards the process as fair if the procedure produces correct outcomes.
2. The balancing model believes a fair procedure is one that reflects a fair balance between the costs of the procedure and the benefits that it produces.
3. The participation model contends a fair procedure is one that affords those who are affected an opportunity to participate in the making of the decision.

Rights

Rights have their origin in secular societal law and are fundamentally limited. Obligations derive from sacred, ethical, and moral codes that are universal to humanity. They are connected through the correlativity thesis.

The correlativity thesis: The strong version of this concept says that rights entail obligations and obligations entail rights. A weaker view claims that rights entail obligations but obligations do not necessarily entail rights.

Rights are classified as positive or negative and are generally exercised by the negation of action.

Positive rights obligate others to act with respect to the right holder. Examples include: the right to counsel, the right to police protection of person and property, the right to public education, as well as rights to food, housing, employment, Social Security, and health care.

Ethics: Theory and Practice

Negative rights forbid others from acting against the right holder. Examples include: freedom of speech, freedom of worship, freedom from slavery, the right to a fair trial, and the right to private property.

Natural rights (also called **moral rights** or **inalienable rights**) are basic rights that are not contingent upon the laws, customs, or beliefs of society and that no government can deny. Unlike legal rights that are culturally and politically relative, natural rights are universal. The modern idea of natural rights grew out of the doctrines of natural law. **John Locke** theorized that individuals have natural rights, such as life, liberty, and property, which are independent of government and society. Locke was influential in the development of liberalism, the belief that political institutions are justified only if they promote human liberty.

Conventional rights are rights that require human agreement. Since legal rights are created through human agreement, legal rights are an example of conventional rights. **Legal rights** are simply rights obtained by being covered by a particular legal system. All legal rights are conventional, but not all conventional rights are legal.

Absolute rights were theorized by Nozick. They are not merely prima facie rights that might be overridden, but boundaries not to be crossed without the free consent of the person whose rights they are. Absolute rights are rights that cannot be interfered with lawfully, no matter how important the public interest in doing so might be. Absolute rights grow from the concept of self-ownership; a person owns his or her own body, and that body's labor, and the fruits of that labor. Nozick posited that absolute rights justified libertarianism, anarchy, and the minimal state.

Liberty

Four principles have been advanced as justifications for legal restrictions on the liberty of individuals:

1. **The harm principle** holds that individual liberty is justifiably limited to prevent harm to others. John Stuart Mill claims that only the harm principle can justify the limitation of liberty. This principle is the most widely accepted.

2. **The principle of legal paternalism** involves the state acting like a parent and forcing the citizen to behave in his/her own best interests by restricting individual liberty. Individual liberty is justifiably limited to prevent harm to self. In modern philosophy

and law, it is described as an act for the good of another person without that person's consent, as parents do for children. At the expense of liberty, paternalists believe they can make better decisions than the people for whom they act. The principle of paternalism can arise in any situation where people hold power over others, such as parenting, education, and medicine. It seems most controversial in cases of criminal law, where the state seeks to protect a person's good by acting to protect the person from him/herself. The state does this coercively, often against a person's will. John Stuart Mill clearly rejects this principle as a basis for limiting liberty.

3. **The principle of legal moralism** involves laws prohibiting what is offensive to the majority of a community, or actions seen as destroying the fabric of a society. It states individual liberty is justifiably limited to prevent immoral behavior. Legal moralism is usually reserved for so-called victimless crimes. If there were victims, the harm or legal paternalist principles might apply. The opinion of the majority of the community is usually used to determine what is moral and immoral. John Stuart Mill rejects this liberty-limiting principle because it represents what he calls the "tyranny of the majority."

4. **The offense principle** believes individual liberty is justifiably limited to prevent offensive behaviors. It is based on three conditions:
    a. The behavior must be significantly offensive to be limited.
    b. The behavior must be offensive to almost everyone.
    c. The offensive act should be limited if you have to go out of your way to avoid the act.

Autonomy

Kant's discussion of the connection between morality and freedom centers on autonomy of the will. He identifies **autonomy** as the supreme principle of morality. His connection between freedom and civil society exists on two levels. First, one precondition of autonomy (i.e. internal freedom) is **liberty** (i.e. external freedom), and an individual can secure his/her liberty only once he/she is a member of civil society. Second, an individual is free only when others recognize him/her as a being with the capacity for autonomous action, and joining civil society is the process by which this recognition takes place. Rather than be defined by external sources, to be autonomous is to be one's own person, to be guided by thoughts, desires, and characteristics that are part of one's authentic self.

Informed Consent

Informed consent is intended to promote and protect the autonomy of health care recipients. **Autonomy** in this context involves the obligation to enable patients to make choices and accept or deny information. For consent to be legally and ethically valid it must be free of **coercion**, (the use of force or restraint). The individual whose consent is being sought must have the ability to make that particular decision, known as **competence**.

Ethics: Theory and Practice

Chapter 7 Review Questions

1. The concept that judges need to be impartial stems from the concept of
    a. Distributive justice.
    b. Retributive justice.
    c. Procedural justice.
    d. None of the above.
2. The right to live free from violent crime would be a
    a. Positive right.
    b. Negative right.
3. The right to be defended in court by an attorney, even if you cannot afford one, is which type of right?
    a. Natural
    b. Conventional
    c. Absolute
4. Seatbelt and helmet laws are examples of
    a. The harm principle.
    b. The principle of legal paternalism.
    c. The principle of legal moralism.
    d. The offense principle.
5. While people have the freedom of speech, people do not have the right to yell "Fire!" in a crowded theater when there is no fire, because such an action would cause people to panic needlessly and rush for the exits; as a result of this pandemonium, people could get trampled and/or experience emotional trauma. This limitation of liberty falls under:
    a. The harm principle
    b. The principle of legal paternalism
    c. The principle of legal moralism
    d. The offense principle

Ethics: Theory and Practice

Chapter 8: Abortion and Euthanasia

Learning Objectives
After reading this chapter, you should be able to:

1. Identify and explain key concepts of the abortion debate.
2. Summarize philosophical and legal views of abortion.
3. Distinguish between types of euthanasia.

Abortion

For the last 40 years the legality of abortion has been a continually argued and controversial topic. Abortion can be defined as the termination of a pregnancy and destruction of the fetus while in the mother's womb.

In one of the most controversial decisions in United States Supreme Court history, **Roe v. Wade** (1973) established that most laws against abortion violate a constitutional right to privacy. This opinion written by **Justice Blackmun** overturned all state laws restricting or outlawing abortion. Roe v. Wade prompted a continuing national debate over whether a state can deem terminating pregnancies illegal if it chooses to do so. Roe v. Wade has reshaped national politics, dividing the nation and inspiring activism.

Pro-life supporters are people who are against abortion completely. Some are opposed for religious reasons, possessing beliefs about the **personhood** of fetal human life. Others view the court's decision as illegitimate because they feel it strayed too far from the text and history of the Constitution.

The *pro-choice* side is comprised of those individuals who believe it is the woman's right to choose whether to have an abortion. Support for Roe v. Wade comes from those who view the decision as necessary to preserve women's equality and personal freedom, and those who believe in the privacy of an individual over collective rights.

The Constitution protects "persons" by granting them rights the states must respect. A core conflict in this debate is the question of when does a new human being exist with full civil rights. One reason for this conflict is the lack of consensus of the exact timing of the beginning of human personhood. It appears impossible for philosophers, religious leaders, medical professionals, or the public to reach a consensus about when personhood begins.

Judith Jarvis Thomson's *A Defense of Abortion* is one of the most influential papers in all of applied ethics, and several of the arguments Thomson makes have become a standard part of the discussion. She believed a fetus is a person and abortion is not presumptively wrong. Her argument is that the burdens of pregnancy are too great of a demand on the rights of a human. A pregnant woman should not be required to act as a **Good Samaritan** to the fetus. Some legal precedents and public opinion support Thomson's conclusion; however, the Good Samaritan reasoning is missing from the Supreme Court's decision about abortion.

Thomson created an analogy to illustrate the moral question. A person wakes up one morning to find that while he was sleeping, someone attached a famous violinist to him, connected by various tubes. The person's body is now the sole support of life for the violinist. If the tubes were to be disconnected, the violinist would die. In order to heal, the violinist needs to stay attached to the person for nine months. During that time the person's body will supply the violinist with all the nutrients and fluids he needs to live, at considerable risk to the person's health. Thomson's violinist scenario implies that the major moral question is whether or not unplugging the violinist is direct killing (where the killing is an end or a means to an end), or self-defense (protecting oneself from physical harm).

Mary Anne Warren, an American writer and philosophy professor, states that a fetus is not a person and abortion is not presumptively wrong. Warren discussed criteria for moral personhood such as consciousness, the ability to reason, the capacity for communication, the ability to have motives and goals, and the ability to have a sense of self. According to Warren, a being doesn't need to exhibit all of these criteria to qualify as a person with a right to life, but if a being exhibits just one or none of them, then it is not a person. According to Warren, a fetus does not meet these criteria; therefore, the fetus is not a person, and abortion is morally permissible.

Other philosophers use criteria similar to Warren's, concluding that a fetus lacks a right to life because it lacks rationality, self-consciousness, or autonomy. These ideas suggest various developed psychological features not found in fetuses, but diverge over exactly which features grant a right to life. There is a full range of plausible options on the issue of whether the fetus is a moral person. For example, **Don Marquis** makes a very unique contribution to the abortion debate. He does not appeal to the idea of personhood or religious premises in his strong anti-abortion position. Instead, Marquis argues that abortion is seriously wrong even if we assume that the fetus is not a person. He suggests that abortion is wrong because it deprives a being of a future.

Euthanasia

Euthanasia refers to the practice of ending life painlessly. The way in which euthanasia is carried out is further defined as:

1. **Voluntary passive euthanasia (VPE)** involves the withholding of treatments (such as chemotherapy or surgery), knowing that this may also result in death (principle of double effect). This is the most accepted form of euthanasia, and is usually done at the request of the patient or the patient's family.
2. **Voluntary active euthanasia (VAE)** entails the use of lethal substances or forces to cause a person's death. It is the most controversial and problematic, and is generally legally prohibited.

The philosophical distinction between **acts and omissions** seems a natural way to distinguish between killing and allowing the natural process of dying. On this account, if a physician does something (e.g. injects an overdose of morphine, which is an action) this should count as VAE. These actions are considered killing, and are generally prohibited. If the physician chooses to do nothing, or to not do something, it is considered VPE. For example, a doctor may choose to not provide essential antibiotics, which is an omission; this would be VPE. These actions are considered to be allowing an individual to die. Some people hold that there is a moral distinction between acts which cause death (active euthanasia) and omissions that cause death (passive euthanasia). Some consider only passive euthanasia to be morally permissible.

Assisted suicide is a form of euthanasia where the patient actively takes the last step in his/her death. This differs from active euthanasia because the "assistant" provides the patient with the means (drugs or equipment) to end his or her own life, rather than ending the life for them.

The Patient Self-Determination Act of 1991 gives every competent adult the fundamental right to self-determination regarding decisions pertaining to his/her own health, including the right to choose or to refuse medical procedures/treatments. In many situations a person may have a **living will**, which is a declaration of desire that life-prolonging measures be provided, withheld, or withdrawn in the event one is determined to have an end-stage condition, is considered terminally ill, or in a persistent vegetative state. These instructions only take effect when the person does not have the capacity to make a medical decision. A person may also appoint a **durable power of attorney for health care**, i.e. a competent adult designated by an individual to make health care decisions on his/her behalf should he/she become incapacitated. These documents have been very instrumental in resolving ethical dilemmas.

Chapter 8 Review Questions

Read the scenario and answer the questions that follow.

Mary is pregnant, single, and believes she is no position to support and raise a child on her own. She is afraid the pregnancy might cause her to be fired from her job, and so is reluctant to go the adoption route. She is considering abortion, and she speaks to various members of her family for advice while weighing her options.

Her aunt Sara said, "You can't get an abortion. You'll be preventing that little person from having a future. He or she could grow up to do great things. Besides, abortion is murder."

Her sister Martha disagreed: "It's not a person yet. The fetus doesn't have the ability to reason or communicate, and it's not self-motivated or self-aware, or even conscious. It's not murder if it's not a person."

Her cousin Lena advised, "It doesn't matter whether it's a person or not. It's your body. If you don't want to have to carry that baby around for nine months, risking your health and your job, you don't have to."

1. Aunt Sara's position is most like that of
    a. Judith Jarvis Thomson
    b. Mary Ann Warren
    c. Don Marquis
    d. All of the above
2. Martha's position is most like that of
    a. Judith Jarvis Thomson
    b. Mary Ann Warren
    c. Don Marquis
    d. All of the above
3. Lena's position is most like that of
    a. Judith Jarvis Thomson
    b. Mary Ann Warren
    c. Don Marquis
    d. All of the above

Ethics: Theory and Practice

Read the following scenarios and answer the questions that follow:

Harold was 89 years old, widowed twice, and suffering from dementia. He broke his hip, had surgery, and then developed pneumonia. He stopped breathing and was put on a ventilator; it soon became evident that it was the only thing keeping him alive. He was not conscious, and so the decision was put to his daughter: should they take him off the ventilator and let nature take its course, or keep him on the ventilator, without any hope of his recovering? His daughter decided to take him off the ventilator.

Sylvia was 92 years old, with a sharp mind, but her body was giving out on her. She had been independent all her adult life, but lately she had needed help getting around town. Her doctor just diagnosed her with a condition that was going to leave her unable to walk, talk or take care of herself any longer; she would have to be totally dependent on someone else, probably in an expensive nursing home that would take all her life savings that she was planning on leaving to her grand-nieces and nephews. She started researching medications on the internet that would let her die by drifting off to sleep. She asked her doctor to prescribe some for her.

A convicted murderer is brought into the prison infirmary; he had been jumped and beaten badly. He had severe internal injuries and shattered bones in addition to his external wounds, and he was in great pain. If he survived this beating, he would suffer from chronic pain and disability for the rest of his life. He had been convicted of murdering several people, and he was serving a 135-year sentence. While administering morphine to the convict, the prison doctor administered three times the recommended dose, and the convict died.

4. Which person participated in assisted suicide?
    a. Harold's doctor
    b. Sylvia's doctor
    c. The prison doctor
    d. All of the above

5. Which person participated in Voluntary Passive Euthanasia?
    a. Harold's doctor
    b. Sylvia's doctor
    c. The prison doctor
    d. All of the above

6. Which person participated in Voluntary Active Euthanasia?
    a. Harold's doctor
    b. Sylvia's doctor
    c. The prison doctor
    d. All of the above

Chapter 9: Animals and the Environment

Learning Objectives
After reading this chapter, you should be able to:

1. Compare and contrast egocentrism and anthropocentrism.
2. Explain land ethic and its criticisms.

Environmental Ethics

Environmental ethics extend the traditional boundaries of ethics to include the non-human world. When studying environmental ethics, the most fundamental question is, "What obligations do we have concerning the natural environment?" If the answer is that we, as human beings, will die if we do not constrain our actions towards nature, then that ethic is considered to be **anthropocentric**. Determining whether our environmental obligations are founded on anthropocentric or non-anthropocentric reasoning will lead to different accounts of what those obligations are.

Anthropocentrism (Ethical Humanism)

The theory of anthropocentrism says that the world exists for humanity. Anthropocentrisms would say that humans have an elevated moral standing and can rightfully try to benefit as much as possible from the environment. Although the history of Western philosophy is dominated by this kind of anthropocentrism, it has many critics. Environmental ethicists claim moral standing should be extended beyond its use to humanity. Some claim this extension should apply to sentient animals, individual living organisms, or holistic entities such as ecosystems. Under these ethics, we have obligations with respect to the environment because we have a moral obligation to the creatures or entities themselves, within the environment.

Biocentrism (Eco-centrism)

The opposite of anthropocentrism is **biocentrism (eco-centrism).** While anthropocentrism argues in favor of a worldview centering solely on humans and only recognizes value in human beings, biocentrism states that everything in nature has value. The Judeo-Christian tradition is blamed by most eco-centrics as the primary source of anthropocentric thought. They are also highly critical of the notion that we should have a greater understanding of nature in order to have greater power over nature. They reject the implication that nature is subservient to man.

Ethics: Theory and Practice

Paul Taylor described the three fundamental points of biocentrism in his book *Respect for Nature*. His arguments are integral to the philosophy of **deep ecology**:
1. People must not harm any part of nature that has inherent value.
2. People must not try to control or change natural ecosystems.
3. People must respect and protect animals.

When applied, these ideas oppose hunting and fishing, and would call for vegetarianism. Taylor diverges from some environmentalists by not placing value on non-living objects in nature.

In 1970, **Richard Ryder** coined the term **speciesism**, which refers to the widely held belief that the human species is inherently superior to other species. Based on this premise, humans have rights and privileges that are otherwise denied to other sentient animals.

Ryder purposely used the term as a wake-up call to challenge the morality of the current practices where non-human animals were exploited in research and farming, domestically and in the wild. Ryder drew a conscious parallel with the terms racism and sexism when coining the term, pointing out that all such prejudices are simply based on physical differences that have little moral relevance. He further asserts that the moral implication of Darwinism is that all sentient animals, humans included, should retain a similar moral status.

Many distinguishing features of humanity (extreme intelligence, complex languages, etc.) are not apparent in marginal cases such as the young or mentally disabled. Because of this, it is apparent that the only distinction for humans to retain superiority over other sentient animals is based on species alone.

Sentience includes the ability to feel or perceive subjectively. Animal rights activists argue that all animals are sentient in that they can feel pleasure and pain. This, in turn, entails the presumption of certain moral rights and ought to entail some legal rights.

According to Princeton University professor **Peter Singer**, the sole criterion for moral standing is sentience. Singer further states that equal consideration does not imply equal treatment. He does not claim that any animal's life is as valuable as any human's life.

According to bioethicist **Bonnie Steinbock**, there are morally good reasons humans are more important than animals, affirming **speciesism**.

Although she does think that the issue of pain in animals should be considered, the issue is not as important as that of human pain. She claims animals have moral status on their own right because they have interests of their own. Beings without interests of their own (such as plants, works of art, embryos) do not have moral status, but if there are moral reasons to protect them, they may have moral value.

This differs from **Peter Singer**'s (animal welfare) view that there is no essential difference between the pain of animals and human beings. This also differs from **William Baxter**'s (anthropocentrism) view that animals have no moral consideration on their own whatsoever. **Instrumental argument**s, such as those put forth by Baxter, claim that animals have rights only insofar as they are of value to us. Animals are viewed as means to our ends of development, interests, or quality of life.

The Land Ethic

Aldo Leopold wrote a famous essay in the 1940s called *The Land Ethic*. In it, he wrote we should think of land as a fountain of energy flowing through soil, water, plants, and animals. Leopold believed the planet was comprised of many systems of life that are intricately woven to function as a whole. All living things were interdependent, creating a community, not a commodity. Humans are members of the community, not masters of it. **Land ethic** (or **eco-holism**) is the belief that a thing is right when it tends to preserve the integrity, stability, and beauty of the biotic community. It is wrong when it does otherwise.

J. Baird Callicott is widely considered to be the leading contemporary exponent of Leopold's land ethic. He concurs with land ethic, which he believes is the most creative, interesting, and practical of the alternatives. He views the environmentalist position as offering a different perspective on such questions as hunting and meat-eating, as well as on the value of non-animal life.

Ethics: Theory and Practice

Chapter 9 Review Questions

1. Using animals to test the safety of cosmetics is evidence of what ethical philosophy?
    a. Anthropocentrism
    b. Bio-centrism
    c. Speciesism
    d. Land ethic
2. Which of the following ethicists would be LEAST likely to object to animal testing for cosmetic safety?
    a. Paul Taylor
    b. Richard Ryder
    c. Peter Singer
    d. Bonnie Steinbock
3. The argument that animals have the same moral rights, and therefore similar legal rights, as humans centers around the concept of
    a. Deep ecology.
    b. Sentience.
    c. Speciesism.
    d. Instrumental arguments.
4. Which of the following ethicists would be LEAST likely to approve of activities such as drilling for oil, fracking for natural gas, and strip mining for coal?
    a. Richard Ryder
    b. Bonnie Steinbock
    c. William Baxter
    d. Aldo Leopold
5. Which of the following ethicists would be MOST likely to approve of using animal organs and fluids in producing medical treatments for humans?
    a. Paul Taylor
    b. Richard Ryder
    c. William Baxter
    d. Aldo Leopold

Chapter 10: Intimate Relationships, Equality, and Discrimination

Learning Objectives
After reading this chapter, you should be able to:

1. Understand the various contemporary views of equality and discrimination.
2. Comprehend Pineau's communication-based model of sexual interaction.
3. Conceptualize English's ideas of obligations between parents and children.
4. Compare and contrast ideas about "unnatural" sex.

Friendship

In her famous essay *What do Grown Children Owe Their Parents?*, **Jane English** argues that there are things that adult children ought to do for their parents, but they do not owe them anything. She characterized friendship not by reciprocity, but by mutuality. She states friends accept what they need and offer what they can give. Friends should not be motivated by gain, but by affection. When friendships end, the duties of friendship also end and any past unrequested sacrifices should not be considered debts. Therefore, the relationship between parents and adult children should be one of friendship. Parental sacrifices should not be motivated by mutual gain and do not result in debt that children must pay as adults.

Natural Law and Sex

St. Thomas Aquinas compared the sexuality of humans to that of other mammals and concluded that what is natural in human sexuality is the desire to engage in heterosexual coitus. He believes that heterosexual coitus was designed by the Christian God to preserve the species; therefore heterosexual coitus is the natural expression of human sexual nature. He believed the penis was designed by God to implant sperm in a woman's vagina for procreation, and any deviation from this was a violation of God's design and unnatural. Therefore, activities such as masturbation, homosexual sex, or fellatio were deemed immoral offenses. Aquinas' criterion for natural is based on the belief that God designed us only to have sexual contact for purposes of procreation.

Ethics: Theory and Practice

Nagel's Secular Philosophy

Both Aquinas and **Thomas Nagel** (b. 1937) assumed that what is unnatural in human sexuality is perverted and that what is unnatural or perverted in human sexuality is simply that which does not conform with, or is inconsistent with, what they each deem as natural human sexuality. Thomas Nagel denies Aquinas' central idea, that in order to discover what is natural in human sexuality we should emphasize what humans and lower animals have in common. He thought in order to discover what is or is not natural, we should seek to find what humans and other animals do not have in common, allowing us to learn the ways in which humans and their sexuality are special. Nagel argues that sexual perversion in humans should be understood as a psychological phenomenon, rather than a matter of physiological and anatomical placement like Aquinas. He argues that human psychology sets us apart from the other animals, and therefore natural human sexuality must acknowledge this.

Nagel proposes that humans mutually responding to each other with sexual arousal are natural to human sexuality. Unnatural or perverted encounters are those where mutual recognition of arousal is absent. Nagel disagrees with Aquinas that homosexual activities, as a specific type of sexual act, are unnatural or perverted, for homosexual sexual acts may very well be accompanied by the mutual recognition of and response to the other's sexual arousal.

Plato

In *Laws*, Plato writes about how opposite-sex sex acts cause pleasure by nature, while same-sex sexuality is unnatural. In *Book Eight* he considers how to have legislation banning illegitimate procreative sex, homosexual acts, and masturbation accepted by society.

Date Rape

Philosopher Lois Pineau wrote a feminist analysis of date rape in which she seeks to replace myths about female provocation and male self-control with a model of communicative sexuality. She claims in **consensual** sex, each partner tries to understand and promote the aims of the other. She argues that this basic understanding is not present in aggressive or coercive sex. According to Pineau we should use a **communicative** model rather than a **contract** model for testing consent. In the contract model, if the person consented, there is no rape; however, the criteria for consent are varied, and the evidentiary standard for proving consent is low. Pineau's position is that, from a woman's point of view, communicative sex must be established to legitimize sex. The presumption is of non-consent; without communicative sex, the act is date rape. Pineau believes that sexual behavior functions like language, and that a communicative model will serve as a background for generating proof of criminal intent needed for legal involvement. She believes that the legal procedures for judging accusations of date rape are biased against the victim of the rape and argues that the process is biased because it makes faulty assumptions about the nature of sex, and the differences between the male and female sexuality. To put her argument succinctly, she is saying that the law implies that women want to be raped and lead men on.

Equality and Discrimination

Where social inequalities exist, different or unequal treatment occurs between groups. This discrimination can serve to reinforce the boundaries that separate the social groups from each other. Equality is the goal of ending different of unequal treatment. The following concepts are related to the discussion of this issue:

1. **Assimilation** is when a person adopts some or all aspects of a dominant culture (such as its religion, language, norms, or values).
2. **Diversity** is a philosophy of inclusion of individuals from a broad spectrum of differences such as race, gender, or country of origin.
3. **Tolerance** is the appreciation of diversity and ability to exercise a fair and objective attitude towards those whose opinions, practices, religion, nationality, and so on differ from one's own.

John Stuart Mill

In 1869, John Stuart Mill and his wife **Harriet Taylor Mill** wrote *The Subjugation of Women,* an essay arguing in favor of **equality** between men and women. In the essay he states that due to the constraints put on them by men, women's value has yet to be discovered. While this is not a novel idea in our time, empowering women was unheard of in Mill's time, and he received a lot of criticism. He believed that each individual should have the right to prove or disprove him or herself to the world.

Mill argued that inequality of women was an idea from the past, based on ideas of gender dominance. He believed that gender discrimination was a hindrance to human development in the modern world. He claimed that relationships between men and women were regulated by injustice, and that treating women as equals would double the effort toward the higher service of humanity.

In the essay, Mill brings up arguments used in favor of keeping women suppressed and then refutes them with historical example. He looks at the traditions of slavery and points to their impact on the issue. Historically it was thought that one sex should be dominant over the other, just as it was once thought that the natural order of life meant that one race of people should be dominant over another. This belief was not held only by the lowly or small thinkers. Mill points out, even Aristotle and Plato believed that slavery was a perfectly logical system for the world to live by.

Mill advocated the equality of men and women under libertarian principles stating that it's unjustifiable to expect one thing of men and to deny that opportunity to women.

Will Kymlicka

Will Kymlicka (b. 1962) maintains that unlike men, women are faced with an unfair choice between their family and their careers. He says that men pursue personal security by increasing their employment skills, and women pursue security by increasing their attractiveness to men. Kymlicka states that society systematically favors men, placing women at a disadvantage because they have to pursue what men are interested in. Kymlicka also offers an important solution to the problem of dominance by men. He says the solution is not ending discrimination, but the presence of power. Equality will require equal opportunity for women to pursue male-defined roles and the ability to create female-defined roles.

Richard Wasserstrom

In 1979, **Richard Wasserstrom** discussed how skin color or genitals would be of no significance in an ideal society. He argues for judgments to be made without regard to difference, viewing everybody and everything as equivalent. Since judgments cannot be made without a commitment to a value, it is impossible to distinguish between modes of life as more or less worthwhile in this view.

Ethics: Theory and Practice

Chapter 10 Review Questions

1. According to Jane English, what is an adult's duty to his/her parents?
    a. The adult child must provide financial support for both his/her parents.
    b. The adult child must provide financial support for one parent after he/she is widowed.
    c. The adult child must see that his/her parents' end-of-life decisions are carried out.
    d. The adult child owes no duty to his/her parents.
2. The following couples have applied for marriage licenses. Which one would Thomas Aquinas approve of?
    a. Edward (age 84) and Edith (age 82)
    b. Jane (age 31) and Janet (age 28)
    c. Leo (age 23) and Laura (age 21)
    d. Martin (age 28) and Mark (age 34)
3. According to Nagel's secular philosophy of sexuality, which behavior would be considered unnatural, and thus perverted?
    a. An elderly couple falling in love
    b. A first date between two gay men
    c. Sex between two consenting adult women
    d. An employer coercing an employee for a sexual encounter
4. Pineau's communicative model of sexuality removes the possibility of
    a. Implied consent
    b. Consensual sex
    c. Romance
    d. Marriage
5. Kymlicka feels that society
    a. Needs to be restructured so that power is distributed equally between the genders
    b. Leaves women with an unfair choice between family and career.
    c. Leaves women at a disadvantage when competing with men.
    d. All of the above

Ethics: Theory and Practice

Chapter 11: Affirmative Action and Free Speech

Learning Objectives
After reading this chapter, you should be able to:

1. Discuss arguments for and against affirmative action.
2. Understand how justice and social utility relate to affirmative action.
3. Comprehend John Stuart Mill's principles related to freedom of speech.
4. Identify moral and legal principles in free speech court cases.

Affirmative Action

The term **affirmative action** refers to policies that seek to promote individuals on the basis of race, ethnicity, or gender in an attempt to promote opportunities for minorities. These policies generally focus on employment, education, public contracting, and health programs. The motivation towards affirmative action has two goals: to maximize diversity in all levels of society, along with its presumed benefits; and to amend perceived disadvantages due to overt, institutional, or involuntary discrimination.

Arguments for and against affirmative action are numerous. Its defenders offer many reasons to justify preference; primarily these reasons have to do with compensatory or **distributive justice**. One argument involves a concept of **reparation**, an aspect of **justice**. However, it is unclear whether or not affirmative action is sufficient compensation for the past wrongs.

Opponents claim affirmative action based on race, gender, or ethnicity is not consistent with justice. By imposing costs disproportionately on disadvantaged white males, affirmative action creates precisely the sort of injustice correctly judged morally wrong in the case of women and minorities. The **social utility** argument implies that the failure of affirmative action to meet the conditions of justice might be outweighed by the important social good it produces. Supporters of affirmative action note the recognized history of **institutionalized limitations** on the affirmative action participants. However, opponents say affirmative action underrates the accomplishments of people who are chosen because of the social group to which they belong rather than their qualifications. They also claim that affirmative action has undesirable side effects, such as undermining the achievements of minorities; encouraging groups to identify themselves as disadvantaged, even if they are not; and increasing racial tension. Furthermore, they contend affirmative action benefits the more privileged people within minority groups at the expense of the less fortunate within majority groups (such as lower-class whites.) For these reasons, affirmative action has been described as **reverse discrimination**, the practice of favoring members of a historically disadvantaged group at the expense of members of a historically advantaged group.

An American philosopher who specialized in ethics, **James Rachels** (1941-2003) defended racial preferences as a way to counterbalance unearned advantages by whites. Given the pervasiveness of racial discrimination, it is likely, he argued, that the superior credentials offered by white applicants do not reflect their greater effort, **desert** (reward or punishment that is deserved), or even ability. Instead, the credentials reflect their mere luck at being born white. He claimed that some white applicants have better qualifications only because they have not had to contend with the obstacles faced by their African American competitors. Rachels thought reverse discrimination might do injustice to some whites. Yet its absence would result in injustices to African Americans who have been unfairly handicapped by their lesser advantages.

Free Speech

John Stuart Mill was a utilitarian; the greatest happiness for the greatest number was his goal. Mill also added that some kinds of happiness were innately greater than other, as was shown by people favoring one over the other. In his work *On Liberty*, Mill argued that free speech is crucial to the greatest happiness for the greatest number. He that restricting free speech prevented knowledge, and that happiness can only be achieved through knowledge. Free speech was necessary to promote knowledge and learning. In *On Liberty*, Mill reviews four distinct grounds he deemed necessary for the mental well-being of mankind, for freedom of opinion, and for freedom to express opinion. They are:

1. To silence a particular opinion is to *assume that opinion is false* or *dangerous*.
2. Minority opinion and majority opinion often *each hold some portion of the truth*. Public discourse is the only way to combine them and get closer to the whole truth. This will allow comparison, extraction of the truth, and the remainder of ideas to be discarded.

These first two grounds beg the question: What if the minority opinion was false and we somehow knew it to be so with certainty, should we then restrict free speech? Mill had two arguments for this, grounds three and four:

3. Mill argued that *silencing opposing opinions will not destroy them*. Rather, it will push them underground, where they will likely convince many ignorant people that they are true. Silenced ideas have the appeal of being dangerous and forbidden. Allowing false opinions to be aired allows the learned to attack and destroy the merit of false opinions publicly. A false opinion which has had its flaws discussed at great length is less likely to be accepted.

4. Mill argued that *if people feel their belief is true, they should welcome opposing ideas*. They should embrace the opportunity to show people what they believe what they do, and how the ideas they believe to be true are better than the alternative ideas. Allowing false ideas to be discussed will do nothing to harm true ideas. He adds that only those who can defend their beliefs truly know them and are not just blindly accepting them. If people cannot defend their true beliefs, accepted truths may be weakened as people forget why they believed them to begin with. This could result in false ideas with clearer reasons for being held overriding older true ideas because people are unable to remember the grounds of their original true ideas.

Related legal precedents include:

1. **Chaplinsky v. New Hampshire (1942)**
   Chaplinsky v. State of New Hampshire was a case decided by the Supreme Court of the United States, in which the court articulated the **fighting words** doctrine, a limitation of the First Amendment's guarantee of freedom of speech. The court ruled that intimidating speech directed as a specific individual in a face-to-face confrontation amounts to "fighting words," and that the person engaging in such speech can be punished if his/her utterance of the words inflicts injury or tends to incite an immediate breach of the peace. Fighting words were deemed not to contribute to the expression of ideas, or possess any social value in the search for truth. Over the past 50 years, however, the court hasn't found the fighting words doctrine applicable in any of the **hate speech** cases that have come before it, since the incidents involved didn't

meet the narrow criteria stated above.

In November 1942, a Jehovah Witness named Walter Chaplinksy was preaching, passing out pamphlets, and calling organized religion a "racket" on a public sidewalk in downtown Rochester. A police officer removed Chaplinsky and took him to police headquarters after a large crowd gathered that began blocking roads and generally causing a scene.

Along the way they met a town marshal, who had earlier warned Chaplinksy to keep it down and avoid causing a commotion. This time, Chaplinsky attacked him verbally by shouting: "You are a God-damned racketeer" and "a damned Fascist." Chaplinksy was arrested and admitted that he said the words charged in the complaint, with the exception of the name of the deity.

Because of this, he was arrested under a New Hampshire statue preventing intentionally offensive speech being directed at others in a public place. Under New Hampshire's Offensive Conduct law
it is illegal for anyone to articulate "any offensive, derisive, or annoying word to anyone who is lawfully in any street or public place…or to call him by an offensive or derisive name." Chaplinksy was fined, but he appealed, claiming the law was "vague" and infringed upon his First and Fourteenth Amendment rights to free speech.

The court, in a unanimous decision, upheld the arrest. The court ruled certain categories of speech fall outside the bounds of constitutional protection. Fighting words were deemed not to contribute to the expression of ideas or possess any social value in the search for truth.

2. Cohen v. California (1968)

In April 1968, Paul Robert Cohen was arrested and convicted for disturbing the peace after he wore a jacket bearing the words "F*** the Draft" in a Los Angeles courthouse. The state argued that the four-letter expletive written on Cohen's jacket was "offensive conduct" that might provoke others to violence against the appellant. Whether Cohen's expression constituted constitutionally protected speech, or fell within the unprotected **fighting words** exception to **free speech** was debated.

The Supreme Court disagreed with the state and reversed the conviction. The court conceded that Cohen's expletive was "vulgar," but it concluded that his speech was nonetheless protected by the First Amendment because it was not an "incitement" to illegal action or an "obscenity." It did not constitute fighting words (personally abusive epithets), since it had not been directed at someone who could not avoid the message or at a person who was likely to retaliate. The court refused to permit the state power to convict on their desire to preserve the cleanliness of discourse in the public sphere. The court stated that no objective distinctions can be made between vulgar and non-vulgar political speech, and that the emotive aspects of speech are often as important as the purely cognitive. Cohen became a landmark decision by expanding the constitutional foundation for protecting provocative and potentially offensive speech.

3. **National Socialist Party of America v. Village of Skokie (1977) (sometimes referred to as the Skokie Affair)**

    The leader of the neo-Nazi group, National Socialist Party of America (NSPA), Frank Collin, proposed a march in Marquette Park on Chicago's southwest side where their headquarters were located. The Park District asked for a huge insurance bond to indemnify them against any damage caused by the anticipated violence, hoping that this requirement would dissuade them from marching. The neo-Nazis then threatened to march in the town of Skokie, a largely Jewish community where some residents were Holocaust survivors. The result was a United States Supreme Court case dealing with freedom of assembly.

    The ACLU sued for the right of the National Socialists to march on behalf of the NSPA. The Illinois Supreme Court did not overrule the county court. It was then brought to the Supreme Court. The Supreme Court ordered Illinois to hold a hearing on their ruling against the Nazis.

    Illinois decided that the county court decision violated the First Amendment. Since other people were allowed to march without paying insurance, the neo-Nazis should be allowed to march as well. An additional question, however, was whether the swastika should be allowed. Concentration camp survivors claimed they did not know if they could control themselves if they saw the swastika in a parade. Skokie attorneys argued that for Jews, seeing the swastika was akin to being physically attacked.

The Illinois Supreme Court sympathized with the Skokie residents, but allowed the National Socialist Party to march anyway. The court ruled that the use of the swastika is a **symbolic expression** of free speech entitled to First Amendment protections and determined that the swastika itself did not constitute **fighting words**. The United States Supreme Court let the Illinois decision stand. The Skokie case shows that the First Amendment guarantees that all views can be expressed regardless of their popularity.

Pornography

The definition of **pornography** has historically been difficult and sometimes controversial. The word itself comes from a Greek word meaning "writing about prostitutes." Some have said this original root word is no longer relevant to the modern usage of the term. However, this is a useful starting point for a modern analysis.

A well-developed definition of **pornography** comes from the feminist analysis of **Helen Longino.** She defined pornography as verbal or pictorial explicit representation of sexual behavior that includes, as a distinguishing characteristic, the degrading and demeaning portrayal of the role and status of the human female as a mere sexual object to be exploited and manipulated sexually.

Under this definition, pornography is one distinct type of sexually explicit material. It is not the sexual content that many feminists object to. It is the advancement of sexual behavior that physically or psychologically violates the personhood of one of the participants.

A related legal precedent includes:

1. **American Booksellers v. Hudnut (1985)**
   In the 1985 case American Booksellers Association v. Hudnut, a federal appeals court struck down the Indianapolis Anti-pornography Civil Rights Ordinance. Pornography, under the

ordinance, was the graphic, sexually explicit subordination of women, whether in pictures or in words, that also includes one or more of the following:

1. Women are presented as sexual objects that enjoy pain or humiliation.
2. Women are presented as sexual objects that experience sexual pleasure in being raped.
3. Women are presented as sexual objects tied up or cut up or mutilated or bruised or physically hurt, or as dismembered or truncated or fragmented or severed into body parts.
4. Women are presented as being penetrated by objects or animals.
5. Women are presented in scenarios of degradation, injury abasement, torture, shown as filthy or inferior, bleeding, bruised, or hurt in a context that makes these conditions sexual.
6. Women are presented as sexual objects for domination, conquest, violation, exploitation, possession, or use, or through postures or positions of servility or submission or display.

The state statute provided that the use of men, children, or transsexuals in the place of women also constituted pornography.

The court ruled that the ordinance violated the First Amendment because it was inconsistent with obscenity doctrine and constituted punishment of speech with a particular viewpoint. In writing an opinion for Miller v. California (1973), Justice Warren Burger wrote that the test for obscenity was "whether the average person, applying contemporary community standards would find that the work, taken as a whole, appeal[ed] to the prurient interest...." Experts pointed to the American Booksellers case as evidence that United States courts, in determining obscenity, still focus on prurience and have refused to make violence or degradation elements of obscenity law.

Chapter 11 Review Questions

1. The theory on which affirmative action is based contends that
    a. By giving preference to traditionally oppressed minorities, we can punish the oppressor.
    b. By maximizing diversity at all levels of society, we can improve social conditions and amend institutionalized limitations.
    c. By lowering standards for employment and education, we create a level playing field.
    d. None of the above
2. According to Mill, why is it important to allow false opinions to be publicly aired?
    a. Suppressing a false opinion makes it seem dangerous and gives it a veneer of credibility; this will give it strength among people who don't actively think for themselves.
    b. Most opposing opinions have some element of truth in them; by discussing opposing ideas, we can learn the truths of both arguments and create a new opinion from it.
    c. Allowing false opinions to be aired gives one the opportunity to defend one's own opinions and test the rightness of one's beliefs. With no opposition to defend against, one cannot be sure one's opinions are true.
    d. All of the above
3. Which one of the following cases reinforced the idea that obscenity was based on prurience alone, and not violence or degradation?
    a. Chaplinksy v. New Hampshire (1942)
    b. Cohen v. California (1968)
    c. National Socialist Party of America v. Village of Skokie (1977)
    d. American Booksellers v. Hudnut (1985)
4. Which one of the following cases set the criteria for judging hate speech cases?
    a. Chaplinksy v. New Hampshire (1942)
    b. Cohen v. California (1968)
    c. National Socialist Party of America v. Village of Skokie (1977)
    d. American Booksellers v. Hudnut (1985)

5. Which one of the following cases established that offensive expression did not fall under the category of "fighting words" or obscenity?
    a. Chaplinksy v. New Hampshire (1942)
    b. Cohen v. California (1968)
    c. National Socialist Party of America v. Village of Skokie (1977)
    d. American Booksellers v. Hudnut (1985)

Appendix A: Overview of Ethical Theories, Theorists, and Terminology

Entries are listed in alphabetical order.

Thomas Aquinas (1225-1274 C.E.) was a Dominican monk who spent his working life studying, teaching, and writing at the University of Paris. His great work, the *Summa Theologica*, unified the **natural law tradition** passed on from the Romans. This was the Biblical tradition through which the Law became identified with the mind of the living God, and the philosophical sophistication of the newly rediscovered work of Aristotle.

Thomas Aquinas believed in the ethics of natural law. It considers that right and wrong, in nature, exists in line with following rationality within society. This ties together the nature of human beings and moral law. The **Principle of Forfeiture** allows a look into how a confrontation of basic values can end. It states that if one threatens another, then the one imposing the harm no longer has rights. This principle goes into further details covering actions of self-defense and those actions taken in war and capital punishment.

Aristotle (382-322 B.C.E.) recorded the first systematic description of virtue ethics in his famous work ***The Nicomachean Ethics***. According to Aristotle, when people are better able to regulate their emotions and their reason, they acquire good habits of character. Aristotle closely observed nature; he believed nature was purposive and did nothing in vain. He also believed if morality refers to our actions, and our actions are a reflection of our beliefs, then morality ought to address what we believe. Aristotle, following Plato, defined the soul as the core or essence of a living being. Although the soul is not a tangible object, it is not separable from the body, in Aristotle's view. By Aristotle's account, the soul has three components: our passion, our faculties, and our states of character. He defines supreme good as an activity of the rational soul in accordance to virtue. According to Aristotle, there are two basic types of virtues: intellectual and moral. He said one should strive to become a virtuous person, and argued that each of the moral virtues was a mean between two corresponding vices.

Axiologically based theories hold that the rightness and wrongness of actions depends entirely on considerations of goodness (value). There are two subtypes:

Consequentialist axiology holds that the rightness and wrongness of actions depends entirely on the goodness (value) of their consequences.

Non-consequentialist axiology holds that the rightness and wrongness of actions does not depend entirely on the goodness (value) of their consequences. These can be further classified into:

> **Strong nonconsequentialist theories** hold that right or wrong do not depend at all on the consequences of actions.
>
> **Weak nonconsequentialist theories** hold that the consequences of our actions are relevant in determining right or wrong but are not decisive.

Jeremy Bentham (1748-1832 C.E.) was a psychological hedonist. He believed that the desire for pleasure and aversion of pain were the only motivation for human actions. He defended the principle of utility and did not promote selfishness. The **Principle of Utility** states that an action is right if it produces at least as much (or more) of an increase in the happiness of all affected by it, than any alternative action. An action is wrong if it does not do this.

Consequentialism, as its name suggests, is the view that normative properties depend only on consequences. This general approach can be applied at different levels to different normative properties of different kinds of things. The most prominent example of this is consequentialism about the moral rightness of an act. This philosophy holds that whether an act is morally right depends only on the consequences of that act. The paradigm case of consequentialism is utilitarianism, whose classic proponents were Jeremy Bentham (1789), John Stuart Mill (1861), and Henry Sidgwick (1907). Classic utilitarianism is consequentialist as opposed to deontological because of what it denies. It denies that moral rightness depends directly on anything other than consequences. The moral rightness of an act depends only on the consequences (as opposed to the circumstances or the intrinsic nature of the act or anything that happens before the act).

Deontological theories hold that the rightness and wrongness of actions do not depend entirely on considerations of goodness (value). Deontology, the science of duty, focuses on the rightness or wrongness of **motives**. The foremost modern defender of this theory is Immanuel Kant insisted that an act cannot be judged right or wrong based on the resulting consequences, which are often out of our hands or a matter of luck, but the principle that guides the action. He felt that people should act with the right intentions, according to the right principles, doing one's duty for its own sake rather than for personal gain and without concern for consequences. Ethics based on deontology is often described as the "ethics of what is right." A deontological ethical decision looks at the problem very differently than teleological theory. It looks at the moral obligations and/or duties of the decision maker, based on principles and rules of behavior. There are two types:

> **Strong deontological theories** contend right or wrong is not dependent on good/bad.
>
> **Weak deontological theories** believe good or bad is relevant to right or wrong but not decisive.
>
> And two subtypes:
>
>> **Rule-based deontology** holds that rightness or wrongness of an action depends on the actions keeping with a rule or rules.
>>
>> **Non-rule based deontology** holds that the rightness or wrongness of an action does not depend on the actions keeping with a rule or rules.
>>
>> The distinction between strong and weak forms for all theories centers on the difference between what is relevant and what is decisive (all else is deemed irrelevant.)

Divine Command Theory is an example of a deontological theory. It actually refers to a cluster of related theories that state an action is right if God has decreed that it is right. The basic tenet is that God's will is the basis of morality.

Emotivism is a non-cognitive theory where value judgments, including moral judgments, do not state facts, but are expressions of emotions or attitudes. It analyzes moral judgments as expressions of unfavorable or favorable emotion.

Entitlement is guarantee of access to benefits because of right or by agreement through law. It is also casually used to refer to the belief that one deserves some particular reward or benefit.

Ethics: Theory and Practice

Epictetus (55-135 C.E.) was an educated, freed slave of Greek origin, who accomplished fame as a Stoic philosopher. **Stoicism** was a school of philosophy during the Roman Empire that emphasized reason as a means of understanding the natural state of things, or logos. It was a means of freeing oneself from emotional distress. No direct known writings of Epictetus survived. The beliefs and thoughts of Epictetus were chronicled by his pupil **Arrian**, in the famous works, ***The Discourses*** and ***The Enchiridion***, or the *The Handbook*.

Epicurus (341-270 B.C.E.) believed in managing one's desires for a balanced life. Focusing on the present and not on an unfortunate occurrence of the future, such as death, will lead to a better life. Epicurus believed the good feelings that come with life are, naturally, the most immediately noticeable; yet, not every pleasure is one in which action is taken. Those actions in which pains occur are not all taken either. There is a balance of times when a painful road is taken in order to later experience a higher level of happiness, which occurs after experiencing pain. Epicurus fully believed prudence is derived from virtues which tie directly with pleasure and one cannot exist without the other.

Ethical Relativism is the concept that what is morally right or wrong may vary fundamentally from person to person or culture to culture. It is supported by the absence of one universal morality in the modern culture.
There are two types of ethical relativism:

1. **Descriptive relativism** notes that there are differences among ethical practices and standards of different cultures, without evaluation of their justification. It is based on empirical fact.
2. **Prescriptive relativism** goes further and claims that people ought not to apply standards of one culture to evaluate the behavior of another culture.

Ethics of care is a normative ethical theory that was developed by feminists in the second half of the twentieth century during the women's movement. While consequentialist and deontological ethical theories emphasize universal standards and impartiality, ethics of care is a **communitarian** approach that emphasizes the importance of relationships. Ethics of care is also a basis for **care-focused feminists** theorizing on maternal ethics. Feminist theorists suggest caring should be performed and care givers valued in both public and private sectors. This proposed paradigm shift in ethics encourages that an ethic of caring be the social responsibility of both men and women. (For more detail, see Chapter 5.)

Existentialism is a philosophy that focuses on finding one's self and the meaning of life through free will, choice, and personal responsibility. Existentialists believe that people are continually searching to discover who and what they are in life as they exercise choices based on their experiences, beliefs, and outlooks. Personal choices are unique and independent of an objective form of truth. An existentialist believes that a person should be required to choose and be responsible without the help of laws, ethnic rules, or traditions. Because existentialist ethics reject the idea of absolute moral laws and most religious-based ethics, it has to find moral significance without these traditional justifications.

Carol Gilligan, a psychologist who studied the differences in morality between the sexes, found that men tended to define morality in more global terms, and women used more affective terms. Her body of work, and others, let to the notion of a **female moral perspective**. This perspective focuses on the context of relationships, emphasizes responsiveness and responsibility to others, and focuses on love, trust, and human bonding.

The Harm Principle holds that individual liberty is justifiably limited to prevent harm to others. John Stuart Mill claims that only the harm principle can justify the **limitation of liberty**. This principle is one of the most widely accepted.

Thomas Hobbes (1588-1679 C.E.) lived in revolutionary times. For the first time in history, Puritan revolutionaries had engineered the overthrow and beheading of the English King, Charles I, in 1641. Hobbes' writing in 1651 had, therefore, a very recent example as motivation for the development of his theory of government. His account of the origin of government in the social contract, later picked up by John Locke and John Rawls as the moral basis of a civil society, is for our purposes, less interesting than his articulation of another notion: the *natural rights* of the citizen as the moral foundation of that government. Self-preservation, and what is needed to achieve this, is seen as the only natural motive when researching the human race. Yet, Hobbes believed in a state where the citizens follow, unquestioningly, the government that allows the people to live in peace and without fear. Hobbes gives an argument for survival: submit to the leader or die, either at the leader's hands or at the hands of your neighbor. Because you value your life, you sign the **social contract** that establishes the **Leviathan**, and obey it until that life is threatened by it. This contract abolishes all other rights. At the point when the government fails to live up to its end of the bargain—protecting the lives of the people—then the people are no longer obligated to support the government.

Jus Ad Bellum: Medieval scholars believed a war could not be entered without certain aspects of the purpose and outcome being met. The doctrine of **jus ad bellum** determines when it is moral to enter a war. The doctrine of **jus in bellum** dictates how a war should be conducted during the course of the conflict. When determining to enter a war, the following guidelines exist: the authority waging the war must be legitimate; all heads of state must be notified of the rules; the war must have just cause, yet be the last resort; peace must be the ultimate goal with success being probable; and the intent for starting the war must not be one of hatred or vengefulness.

Immanuel Kant (1724-1804 C.E.) paved a new way for the thought processes of ethics. He did not take the standard role many before him did; instead, he chose to question, as did Socrates, the wrongness of human acts. Humans are able to choose and judge what actions they take for rightness. When one chooses to commit a wrongful act, that person will not be looked upon favorably.

In one of Kant's writings, he describes and distinguishes between what is good, and what is not good, and the factors that determine this. He believed good will is the only good that is without qualification in existence, while explaining how something can only be good if it is compatible with good itself. Kant helped to relate this in regards to one performing a duty out of duty or just doing it for no other purpose. This, in turn, is what makes a good person good. In addition, it is the presence of self-governing reason—**autonomy**—in each person that Kant thought offered decisive grounds for viewing each individual as possessed of equal worth and deserving of equal respect.

Ethics: Theory and Practice

Kantianism is a deontological, act-based, human valuing philosophy. Kant believed people were inherently bad and that we needed to use our reason to come up with a moral framework to transcend mortal life and ultimately gain entrance to heaven. To do this, people have to live by acts that are as selfless as possible. Kant's **Categorical Imperatives** are maxim-based obligations for moral reasoning and behavior. The first three formulations of Kant's Categorical Imperatives are discussed in detail in Chapter 4.

Martin Luther King, Jr. (1929-1968 C.E.) built on the themes that have been with us since Epictetus. From the Stoics, there is disdain for the punishments, including fetters and prisons, that the unjust world visits upon the just man in the attempt to silence him. From Thomas Aquinas, citing Augustine (as does King), there is the certainty that the unjust law is no law at all, and should in no way be obeyed. From Thomas Hobbes, John Locke, and Thomas Jefferson, the willingness not only to assert constitutional rights, but to insist that they be incorporated into the law of the land, in this case, all the lands of the United States. We may add, from Jefferson, the acceptance of a certain quota of violence as the cost of liberty; from Kant, the centrality of the notion of human dignity; from Josiah Royce, the fierce devotion to that cause which fulfilled and consumed his life; and from Rawls, his contemporary, the recognition that peace and plenty are worthless without justice.

Individual liberty it justifiably limited to prevent harm to self. In modern philosophy and law, it is described as "an act for the good of another, without that person's consent," as parents do for children. At the expense of liberty, **paternalists** believe they can make better decisions than the people for whom they act. The principle of paternalism can arise in any situation where people hold power over others, such as parenting, education, and medicine. It seems most controversial in cases of criminal law, where the state seeks to protect a person's good by acting to protect the person from him/herself. The state does this coercively, often against a person's will. John Stuart Mill clearly rejects this principle as a basis for limiting liberty.

Legal Paternalism: This principle involves the state acting like a parent and forcing the citizens to behave in their own best interests by restricting liberty.

Ethics: Theory and Practice

John Locke (1632-1704 C.E.) comes from a different revolution than Hobbes. Shortly after Hobbes wrote, monarchy was restored. When it threatened to become inconvenient again, the English Parliament lost patience with their king, threw him out of the country, and invited Prince William of Orange, Prince of the Netherlands, to be their king. He was a good king. More to the point, Parliament had established that it and it alone, was the representative of the people, and had the right to control succession to the English throne. Despite all the flaws of democracy of the time, England was firmly in democratic hands. Locke's writings celebrate that revolution, the Glorious Revolution of 1688.

In his political theory, Locke carries on from Hobbes. Locke presented a gentler view of human nature, but with man of the same assumptions about human motivation and the consequences for human action. The primary objective of the social contract for Locke is the protection of property. In protection of property, he includes our notions of life and liberty (for a man's body and freedom are, after all, his own). Life and liberty are most endangered, in the state of nature, in the form of physical property and its enjoyment. We need a civil society primarily for the safety of lands and industry; settling boundaries, setting regulations, and establishing judges for the inevitable disputes. Here the fundamental rights of the human being—life, liberty, and property— are established, along with the role of law in protecting those rights.

John Stuart Mill (1806-1873 C.E.) was a utilitarian. The greatest happiness for the greatest number was his goal. Mill also added that some kinds of happiness were innately greater than others, as was shown by people favoring one over the other. In his work *On Liberty*, Mill argued that free speech is crucial to the greatest happiness for the greatest number. He thought that restricting free speech prevented knowledge, and that happiness can only be achieved through knowledge. Free speech was necessary to promote knowledge and learning.

Moral Justification: The word *justification* is commonly used in two different senses, one positive and the other negative. The **negative sense** is the one which is typically accompanied by an accusation that the justifier is being insincere. It is, in this sense, that fast-talkers are sometimes accused of being able to *justify* anything and everything. The **positive sense** of justification, on the other hand, involves bringing others to see our actions as reasonable. In this sense, a course of action is justified if there are better reasons in favor of it than there are against it. Preferably, these reasons should be ones that other people could agree are good ones. It is this sense of justification that is important for morality. **Moral justification,** then, means showing that there are more or better moral reasons for a course of action than against it.

Moral legalism holds that the moral rightness of acts is determined solely by rules, principles, or commandments. Moral legalism can be either consequentialist or non-consequentialist in perspective.
Examples of **moral legalism** (discussed in other chapters) are:

1. Kantianism – One ought always to act on maxims that can be universal.
2. Ethical egoism – One ought to always act to maximize one's personal good.
3. Divine Command Theory – Whatever God commands is right.
4. Principle of Justice – One ought always to act justly.
5. Natural Law Ethics – One ought always to act in accordance with nature.
6. Utilitarianism – One ought to always act to maximize the general good.

Moral particularism contends moral principles are secondary to outcomes. The rightness of an act depends solely on the situations in which it is performed, and is not derived from rules, principles, or commandments. Moral particularism is predominantly consequentialist by may be guided by moral principles.

Natural Law Theory: The term natural law is ambiguous. It refers to a type of moral theory, as well as to a type of legal theory, but the core claims of the two kinds of theory are logically independent. According to **natural law moral theory**, the moral standards that govern human behavior are, in some sense, objectively derived from the nature of human beings and the nature of the world. While being logically independent of **natural law legal theory**, the two theories intersect. The first is a theory of morality that is roughly characterized by the following theses:
First moral propositions have, what is sometimes called objective standing, in the sense that such propositions are the bearers of objective truth-value. Moral propositions can be objectively true or false.

Ethics: Theory and Practice

The second thesis constituting the core of natural law moral theory is the claim that standards of morality are, in some sense, derived from the nature of the world, and the nature of human beings.

Thomas Aquinas, for example, identifies the rational nature of human beings as that which defines moral law: *the rule and measure of human acts is the reason, which is the first principle of human acts.*

According to natural law legal theory, the authority of legal standards necessarily derived, at least in part, from considerations having to do with the moral merit of those standards. **Classical natural law theory**, such as the theory of Aquinas focuses on the overlap between natural law moral and legal theories.

Plato (424-348 B.C.E.) uses the myth, **The Ring of Gyges**, to illustrate the concept of morality and egoism in his book, ***The Republic***. To Plato, the soul has three parts: desire, spirit, and reason. Plato, following the ideas of his teacher, Socrates, considered the soul as the essence of people, and responsible for deciding how we behave. Plato considered the soul to be an eternal occupant of our being that is continually reborn in subsequent bodies after our death. The **Platonic soul** is made up of three parts: the logos (mind), thymos (emotion), and eros (desire). Each part has a specific defined function in a balanced and peaceful soul. Plato saw the soul as a ghostly occupant of the body.

John Rawls (1921-2002 C.E.) attempted to associate Kantian philosophy with the law. Unlike Kant, he was concerned with the issue of fairness and social justice. He developed a social contract theory of justice. Social contract describes a broad class of theories that try to explain the ways in which people form state and/or maintain social order.

Rawls believed in a fair viewpoint of justice regarding each member of society, in which social cooperation is followed by a form of established government. In advance, the members of this hypothetical society are to decide what is acceptable, determining the principles of justice. The thought is that no one knows the details of their societal standing. This **veil of ignorance**, the key concept of this scenario, allows for judgments to be impartial.

Jean-Jacques Rousseau (1712-1778 C.E.) attempts to thread a path between the philosophies of Hobbes and Locke, trying to solve the problem of legitimacy in organized human society. Hobbes gives an argument for survival: submit to the social contract, and relinquish any other rights.

Locke preserves rights, and supports very limited government that operates by majority vote, limiting the Ruler. Can majorities be speculatively wrong? Is every majority vote legitimate? Lock has to say yes, allowing only for a written constitution (also terminable by the majority) to protect us from the mob.

Rousseau sees that, while either of these schemas can work (both have), both are legitimate only by chance. Rousseau insists that Society, the product of the first unanimous Contract, carries the true will of the people, the **General Will**. The General Will is distinct from the State, a product of a majority vote, which can only give us the Will of All. According to Rousseau, therefore, Locke is wrong in his insistence that the majority is always right, or at least that there is no conceivable power to place against the majority, and Hobbes is wrong in his abandonment of liberty in the name of security.

Even though Rousseau and Hobbes did agree on some political issues, they did not agree on the aspect of the **social contract**. Hobbes believed in following the social contract of the ruler until one's life is threatened. While Rousseau states an understanding of this notion, he believed that people should follow their free will, which allows for everyone's freedom. This equates to the existence of people within a community and what kind of solidarity they can create within a community.

Socrates (469-399 B.C.E.) was an ancient Greek philosopher who is widely credited for laying the foundation for **western philosophy**. By far the most important source of information about Socrates is Plato, who depicts him as a contradictory character. Plato's dialogues feature Socrates, a teacher who denies having disciples, as a man of reason who obeys a divine voice in his head, and a pious man who is executed for religious improprieties. Socrates disparages the pleasures of the senses, yet is excited by youthful beauty. He is devoted to the education of the boys of Athens, yet indifferent to his own sons; few other characters have so fascinated the western world.

The trial and execution of Socrates was the climax of his career and the central event of the dialogues of Plato. According to Plato, however, both were unnecessary. Socrates admits in court that he could have avoided his trial in the first place by abandoning philosophy, and going home to mind his own business. After his court conviction, he could have avoided the death penalty by agreeing to pay a small fine, and one in prison, he could have escaped. Socrates participated in his famous martyrdom every step of the way, and his story supplies, one way or the other, the foundation for western philosophy.

Socrates: The Crito is one of four stories that tells of Socrates' trial and death and describes why he stood by his reasoning for not escaping from prison. Escaping from prison was not unheard of during the days of Athens, so Socrates' friend, Crito, cane to see him with a plan on how to do so. Socrates explained to Crito why he must abide by the laws of Athens even when applied unjustly. Keep in mind that Socrates believed that harming a person meant making him less good, less virtuous, less excellent. Thus, a person is harmed by making him less just or good. Thus, as long as you retain your virtue, you are not harmed. This is why, for Socrates, it was better to suffer an injustice than to do one. By suffering an injustice, one does not show one's self to be vicious (without virtue); by doing an injustice, one does show one's self to be vicious. Crito gave three arguments as to why Socrates should escape. They were: not escaping would harm Socrates' friends because they would be ridiculed for lacking the courage to help him escape and their reputations would suffer; not escaping would make it impossible for Socrates to provide for his children; and not escaping would make it impossible for Socrates to continue to teach philosophy, therefore his enemies would have won.

Socrates, in turn, replied in defense of himself. He accepted the principle that one ought not to harm one's friends. So long as Socrates did not lead his friends to commit an injustice, he did not harm them. One must first determine whether escape is unjust; if it is, then by allowing his friends to help him escape, Socrates would be truly harming them. Socrates' defense for Crito's second argument was that one benefits one's children by making them just and virtuous. If escaping is unjust, and Socrates escaped, then he would show himself unfit as a teacher of virtue—he would have shown that he did not know what virtue is, and so he could not make his children just or virtuous. Socrates' final argument was that if he, Socrates, wanted to teach philosophy, he must not show himself to be ignorant of virtue. Socrates believed that knowledge is virtue, to know the good is to do the good. If he acted wrongly, he would have shown that he had no knowledge to give to others.

Teleological Moral Theory can be described as the "ethics of what is good." A teleological ethical decision considers rightness or wrongness, based on the outcomes of that decision. Teleological moral theory is any moral theory that is both axiological and consequential. The principle forms of this theory are:

> **Micro ethics** is concerned with the good of the group when the good is the good of the individuals that make up the group.
>
> **Macro ethics** values the survival and well-being of individuals, groups, and entities (such as nature). The good of the whole does not necessarily relate to the good of the parts.

Utilitarianism is one example of a consequentialist moral theory. At the core of utilitarianism is the **Principle of Utility** or the **Greatest Happiness Principle**. An **ethical decision** is one that offers the greatest net utility: the greatest amount of happiness for the greatest number of people. See Chapter 3 for a more extensive discussion.

Virtue Ethics places an emphasis on *who you are* rather than on *what you do*. Morality stems from the identity and/or character of the individual, rather than the belief that, in order to live a moral life, one must begin by developing good character. We, therefore, ought to act in ways that exhibit virtues (such as courage or compassion), even if that means doing what might generally be seen as bad or bringing about undesirable consequences.

Appendix B: Ethical Analysis of Issues and Practical Applications

Relationships and Sexuality

Sexual ethics (sometimes called sexual morality), addresses the ethical concepts that are involved in issues that may arise from all aspects of sexuality and human sexual behavior. In general, sexual ethics deals with the community and personal standards which influence one's behavior in interpersonal relationships. It also impacts issues of consent, sexual relationships before marriage or while married, questions about sexual behavior can be used to reflect gender and power, and how individuals relate to society.

Ethical dilemmas involving sex are often seen in situations where there is a considerable power difference between the participants, or where the issue of consent is uncertain.

Flirting occurs when one person evasively indicates a romantic and/or sexual interest toward another. This can involve body language, conversation, joking, or brief physical contact. This poses an ethical dilemma because it can be misinterpreted as more serious, or it may be thought of as cheating if the person is already in a romantic relationship.

Premarital sex is an issue often debated on the basis of religious or moral grounds. It involves young people engaging in sexual activity before their marriage.

Extramarital sex occurs when married people become sexually involved with someone other than their marriage partner. Some regard this as **adultery**; others regard it as **infidelity** or as **cheating**. Adultery may be thought to be seriously wrong because it involves the breaking of a promise. Since it also involves deception, and deception is wrong, so is adultery. Some cultures, however, accept extramarital sex as the norm. Some modern western cultures practice **polyamory**, also known as responsible non-monogamy, or open-marriage. This ethical practice can only work with honest dialogue, and consent of the parties involved—including spouses.

Consent is a central issue in sexual ethics. Children, the mentally challenges, the mentally ill, and sometimes people under the influence of drugs or alcohol are considered as lacking the ability to give an informed consent. Illegal sexual acts are also considered unethical, because of the absence of consent, including rape and molestation.

Date rape is a non-aggravated sexual assault. It is **nonconsensual** sex that does not necessarily involve physical injury or the threat of physical injury. The problem with pressing charges in these cases is the criterion for consent, which says that consent is implied unless some emphatic episodic sign of resistance occurred and its occurrence can be established.

Sexual harassment: Most societies do not condone a person in a position of power engaging in sexual activity with a subordinate. This is unethical in that it is a breach of trust. Using one's position of power in the workplace may constitute sexual harassment, because subordinates might be too afraid of repercussions to give proper consent to sexual advances.

Pornography

As a basic human drive, sex can be used toward unethical ends. Sex, in the form of sex work or pornography, can be exchanged for money in various places. Some feminists contend that this industry exploits women, and is a way of maintaining patriarchy; that prostitution is a form of male domination and oppression of women. Immanuel Kant proposed that some sexual practices violate the basic ethical principle that we must never treat another person only as a means, but always as an end.

Pornography is the verbal or pictorial representation of sexual behavior in an explicit way. It can be a degrading and demeaning portrayal of the role and status of women as sex objects to be exploited and manipulated sexually. In some pornography, women are characterized as slavishly dependent on men. The role of the female is depicted as one simply to provide sexual services to men. Sometimes, in violent pornography women are bound, tortured, gang-raped, mutilated, killed, or abused in many other ways as a means of providing sexual stimulation or pleasure to men.

Whether material is pornography depends on its contextual feature. Not all sexually explicit material is pornographic. What makes it pornographic is its implicit, or even explicit, approval of sexual behavior that is immoral, i.e., that physically or psychologically violates the personhood of the participants in such a way as to endorse degradation.

Public Health

If public health is a major concern, one has to ask whether individuals have an ethical responsibility to the public at large for their behavior. This might include responsibility to use safe sex practices, providing information of infection with sexually transmitted diseases, the ethics of sex without using contraception resulting in an increase in the number of unplanned pregnancies and/or unwanted children, and what each individual needs to do to contribute to the general health of the public.

The ethics of **smoking** have become a vital issue of public health. In this day and age, we can say that everyone is aware of the health risks from smoking. The question is whether the active participation of the smoker really implies voluntary acceptance of the consequences, i.e., the risks of illness and death. This is again a matter of informed consent; does this individual know what any other reasonable person would know regarding the risks of smoking? One argument says that cigarette smoking is addictive, rather than just a habit. That does not mean that no one can quit; many have done so; but it does bring into question the voluntary choice, no matter how well informed. There might have been consent at first, but after an individual is hooked, the capacity to consent in any meaningful sense on a continuing basis is lost.

Surrogate motherhood is an issue that has presented many unique ethical concerns. Some ethicists believe that surrogacy is ethically unacceptable because it is inconsistent with human dignity that a woman should use her uterus for financial profit, and it is exploitive because it's really child-selling. Also, they claim that knowing that a woman is doing this to deliberately give up the child distorts the relationship between mother and child. Some other ethicists conclude that these reasons justify putting restrictions on surrogate contracts, as opposed to banning surrogacy. Others claim they can rebut each of these arguments. For example, some say that respect for individual freedom necessitates that we allow people to make choices they may later regret; or, people often do many risky things for money (race car driving, bungee jumping, sky diving). Usually surrogates choose this role because they enjoy being pregnant and the fee does provide economic compensation, which is better than alternative occupations. Many derive a feeling of self-worth because they think of this as an altruistic act. If these are the intent and motives, then it seems unlikely that the surrogate is being exploited.

Surrogates agree to be impregnated, to carry the child to term, and to provide a couple with a child they could not otherwise have. Children are not property and hence cannot be bought or sold.

The surrender of the child is the whole point of the agreement, and therefore this cannot be considered child-selling.

Physician-assisted suicide is a form of euthanasia where the patient actively takes the last step in his/her death. As opposed to active euthanasia, with physician-assisted suicide, a doctor gives the patient a prescription for drugs that the patient can use to end his/her life, but the main difference is that in this situation the doctor is not the person who actually administers the drug. This can be only considered as an option by a patient who is conscious and capable of making an informed medical decision. The basic moral objection here is that this violates the physician oath to *do no harm*. Some argue that it violates the oath to *do no harm* if a physician prolongs the life of a suffering person. Oregon is the only state that allows physician assisted suicide. The

Oregon Death with Dignity Act (ODWA) was passed in 1994, but went into effect in 1997, and legalized this practice.

For Oregon residents to be able to ask for a prescription under the ODWDA, the following must be present:

- There must be a diagnosis from their primary care physician that states that they have an incurable and irreversible disease that will likely cause their death within six months.
- The physician must determine that the patient has made a voluntary and informed request, and refer patients to counseling if there is any question that a psychological disorder may be impairing their judgment.
- The patient and his/her medical record must be examined by a second physician to confirm the primary care physician's

conclusions. Oregon physicians may prescribe, but may not administer, the requested drug.

The Patient Self-Determination Act of 1991 gives every competent adult the fundamental right to self-determination regarding decisions pertaining to his/her own health, including the right to choose or to refuse medical procedures or treatments.

With the rapidly increasing technological advances and medical knowledge, options for healthcare become more complex. There are many ethical dilemmas when decisions must be made concerning the care of a dying patient. What is the best treatment to ease a patient's suffering at the end of life? Should all treatments be withheld or withdrawn? What about burden vs. benefit?

One cannot entertain a discussion about end of life care without defining the end of life, i.e., death. Death is that point in time when our vital functions cease. Advances in life support, however, have blurred the line between who is alive and who is dead. Therefore, we need specifics that allow us to declare a person physically or legally dead. The **Uniform Determination of Death Act (UDDA) of 1981** confronted these complexities. It specifically states, "An individual who has sustained either (1) irreversible cessation of circulatory and respiratory functions, or (2) irreversible cessation of all functions of the entire brain, including the brain stem, is dead."

Ethical Decisions Surrounding Major Types of Medical Care
Resuscitation

Some terminally ill patients may decide that, should a cardiac event occur, they do not want to be resuscitated. They would ask their physician for a **Do-Not-Resuscitate (DNR) Order**.

Physicians have the ethical obligation to honor their patient's wishes regarding resuscitation. DNR orders might be granted for:

- Patients for whom CPR would not provide any benefit;
- Patients who could have permanent damage, unconsciousness, and poor quality of life if they survived CPR; or
- Patients whose quality of life is poor and who wish to forego CPR in the event that breath or heartbeat cease.

Mechanical ventilation is the most common form of life support that is withdrawn when death is imminent. Mechanical ventilation involves tubes inserted through the nose or mouth into the trachea, and through a machine, where a patient's lungs are inflated and emptied, and allowing oxygenation of the blood. Some care providers consider mechanical ventilation as death-delaying, rather than life-prolonging. Patients, nevertheless, can decide that this is an intervention they do or do not want during their final days.

Hospice Care
Hospice care, a holistic and philosophical approach to end of life care, emphasizes pain control, symptom management, natural death, quality of life, and providing physical comfort for the patient. Unfortunately, access to hospice services is not fair and equitable in the United States. This is partially due to governmental limitations on reimbursement to hospice organizations for Medicare patients. Some hospice programs might also ask patients to sign agreements that they must stop any curative treatments. Hospice also requires that patients have a prognosis of six months or less to live to qualify for hospice care.

Some ethical questions concerning prognosis are:

1. **Accuracy**: Considering the unpredictability of disease, and the vast number of unknown variables that can influence how and when a person will die, it is most quite difficult to come up with an accurate prognosis.
2. **Six-month limitation**: This requirement leaves out people who are near the end of life, but might have longer than six months to live. These individuals would be able to benefit from the hospice team and the many services it could offer.
3. **Prognosis communications with patient**: It may be unethical to expect a physician to make a prognosis and inform the patient, if the patient's culture does not embrace full and open discussion between doctors and patients about healthcare or death.
4. Pain Management: Many ethical dilemmas stem from the use of pain-relieving drugs in terminally ill patients. Some people caution about the fear of addiction to narcotics, about the value of individual autonomy, and about the importance of treating symptoms. Morphine is the most commonly used narcotic for treating pain and other symptoms of the seriously ill. It is especially helpful at relieving the two most common symptoms experienced by dying patients: pain and shortness of breath. Some physicians are worried that the respiratory depression, a side effect of the morphine, may cause death, so they under-

prescribe the drug, even for terminally ill patients who are in extreme pain. Research, however, has not found that narcotics shorten life or depress respiration in dying patients, even when given in high doses.

5. Nutrition and Hydration: Some of the most emotionally and ethically challenging issues in end of life care relate to decisions about nutrition and hydration. This is primarily because of the nature and social meaning attached to providing people with food and water. The United States Supreme Court ruled in 1990 that, legally, artificial nutrition and hydration are not different than other life-sustaining treatments.
6. United States courts have made the following rulings:
7. Competent adults can refuse these treatments, even if this choice hastens their death.
8. A health care surrogate may withdraw these treatments,
9. A health care surrogate may refuse these treatments on behalf of an incompetent adult.

The second debate focuses on whether withholding food and water is similar to killing a patient or allowing a patient to die. Patients, families, and physicians need to come together to determine if this will be beneficial or burdensome to the patient. It should provide the patient with benefit that is enough to outweigh the burdens. This is called the principle of proportionality.

10. Antibiotic Treatments: Many dying patients are susceptible to infection, often because of several co-morbid conditions. Antibiotics obviously won't cure the underlying terminal disease, but may relieve distressing symptoms. Some physicians think that antibiotics are considered part of routine care. Others believe that an infection is a treatable condition and not related to the untreatable terminal illness, and hence find it difficult to withhold antibiotic treatment.
11. Medical Futility: Medically futile treatments are those procedures or interventions that are highly unlikely to benefit a patient. The concept of medical futility leads to many ethical questions. First, can we prevent medical futility from becoming a judgment call made by the health care staff? Second, the fear that some treatments that health care professionals deem not beneficial may actually be considered beneficial by patients, and these may be eliminated. Third, and most important, is that necessary treatments will be labeled as futile to save money.
12. Terminal Sedation: Terminal sedation uses sedatives to make a patient unconscious when death from the underlying disease is imminent. This may be the only way to relive the agonal suffering, the profound pain that may occur when a patient is dying. Since terminal sedation is a risky treatment, some bring up ethical questions about its use, including:
13. Terminal sedation may have an unknown effect on hastening death.

Ethics: Theory and Practice

14. Patients who are unconscious and cannot speak for themselves are at potential risk for abuse.
15. How does one value consciousness vs. suffering?
16. Is using terminal sedation for patients who really don't need such potent relief ethical?
17. How far should people go to attempt to relieve pain and other uncomfortable symptoms?

18. Advance Directives
19. In order to avoid ethical conflicts related to withholding or withdrawing treatments and to encourage the appropriate care of those nearing the end of life, patients are asked to draw up an Advance Directive or Living Will.
20. An Advance Directive or Living Will is a document used to:

21. State the patient's own goals and wishes with regard to medical care;
22. Give specific instructions about treatments, including DNR orders, organ donation, feeding tubes, etc.; and
23. Designate a power of attorney for healthcare who will speak for this person should be/she become unable to express his/her own wishes.
24. Unfortunately, advance directives and living wills are tools that are underused. Many who need them don't have them; sometimes, even when patients have them, they are not followed. Physicians may believe that following these directives would not be in the best interest of the patient.

All states legally recognize some form of advance directives. The Patient Self-Determination Act (PSDA) requires health care facilities receiving federal funding to provide education to the community about advance directives. The PSDA specifically requires health care providers and health care organizations to:

1. Provide written information to all adult patients explaining their rights under state law to make health care decisions, including their right to make an advance directive and how the facility implements them.
2. Document the presence of an advance directive in the patient's medical record.
3. Provide education for staff and family about advance directives.
4. Do not discriminate against patients, or condition care, based on advance directives. The following are some ethical concerns raised about the use of advance directives:
    a) These may improperly influence health care providers to

limit care, leading to under-treatment.
  b) A person who is afraid of becoming disabled may use an advance directive to limit treatment. Realistically, people cannot know in advance how they would cope with and adapt to living with a disability.
  c) Advance directives are time consuming for healthcare professionals, and might not be helpful if a treatment decision requires an answer right away.

Defective Newborns and the Morality of Termination
Many ethical dilemmas arise when it comes to decisions about terminating the life of a defective newborn, or simply letting it die. The questions, which no ethicist can answer, are:
1. What defects would warrant termination?
2. How serious must these defects be?
3. How can anyone make a determination of the quality of life these children would have?

Some physicians feel they would be doing the child a favor by terminating what they would consider a bad life. Having no specific guidelines, physicians will continue to find this decision one of the most difficult they will ever have to make.

Economic Inequity, Poverty, and Equal Opportunity
John Rawls contends that it is not individual relationships, but the major institutions in society that are the first subject of justice. These institutions, which he calls the **basic structure** of society, include society's constitution, federal and state laws, financial markets, and the family. He argues that the basic structure allows for considerable social and economic inequalities, depending on social origin, natural talents and abilities, and the opportunities that have shaped someone's life. The theory of justice must regulate these inequalities in life.

Where social inequalities exist, different or unequal treatment occurs between groups. This discrimination can serve to reinforce the boundaries that separate the social groups from each other. Equality is the goal of ending different or unequal treatment.

The following concepts are related to the discussion of this issue:

1. **Assimilation** is when a person adopts some or all aspects of a

dominant culture, such as its religion, language, norms, or values.
2. **Diversity** is a philosophy of inclusion of individuals from a broad spectrum of differences, such as race, gender, or country of origin.
3. **Tolerance** is the appreciation of diversity, and the ability to exercise a fair and objective attitude toward those whose opinions, practices, religion, nationality, etc., differ from one's own.

In 1869, **John Stuart Mill** and his wife **Harriet Taylor Mill** wrote *The Subjugation of Women*, an essay arguing in favor of equality between men and women. Mill stated that due to the constraints put on them by men, women's value had yet to be discovered. His thinking was ahead of his time. Empowering women was unheard of in his day. He believed that inequality of women was based on ideas of gender dominance and that gender discrimination was a hindrance to human development in the modern world. He claimed that relationships between men and women were regulated by injustice, and that treating women as equals would double the effort toward the higher service of humanity. Mill advocates the equality of men and women under libertarian principles, stating that it is unjustifiable to expect one thing of men and to deny that opportunity to women.

The Equal Pay Act of 1963 stated that men and women doing the same jobs must receive equal pay. The **Lilly Ledbetter Fair Pay Act of 2009** states that the 180-day statute of limitations for filing an equal-pay lawsuit regarding pay discrimination resets with each new paycheck affected by that discriminatory action.

According to **Will Kymlicka**, **sex discrimination** is seen as the arbitrary or irrational use of gender when making decision about benefits or positions. Since the problem in society is still, to some extent, a problem of male domination, the solution then would not be only the absence of discrimination, but the presence of power. Equality demands the opportunity to pursue male-defined roles, but also equal power to create female-defined roles, or to create neutral roles that both men and women would have an interest in pursuing.

Racism and Affirmative Action

The **Civil Rights Act of 1964** outlawed discrimination in employment based on sex, race, color, religion, or national origin.

Ethics: Theory and Practice

The term **affirmative action** refers to policies that seek to promote individuals on the basis of race, ethnicity, or gender in an attempt to promote opportunities for minorities. The motivation toward affirmative action has two goals:

1. To maximize diversity in all levels of society, along with its presumed benefits
2. To amend perceived disadvantages due to overt, institutional, or involuntary discrimination

Arguments for and against affirmative action are numerous. Its defenders base their focus on compensatory of distributive justice. One argument involves the concept of reparation, an aspect of justice. It is unclear, however, if affirmative action is sufficient compensation for past wrongs.

Opponents claim affirmative action based on race, gender, or ethnicity, is not consistent with justice. By imposing costs disproportionately on white males, affirmative action creates precisely the sort of injustice correctly judged morally wrong in the case of women and minorities.

The **social utility argument** implies that failure of affirmative action to meet the conditions of justice might be outweighed by the important social good it produces. Opponents say that affirmative action underrates the accomplishments of people who are chosen because of the social group to which they belong, rather than their qualifications. Furthermore, they contend that affirmative action benefits the more privileged people within minority groups, at the expense of the less fortunate within majority groups, such as lower-class whites.

For these reasons, affirmative action has been described as **reverse discrimination**, the practice of favoring members of a historically disadvantaged group at the expense of members of a historically advantaged group.

Punishment

Martin Perlmutter proposes that there are two aspects of punishment that are essential:

1. Punishment is inflicting harm; it is not really punishment if it is not a deprivation, or does not cause pain or suffering, or have unpleasant consequences. Punishment aims to make a person worse off than he would be without punishment.

2. Punishment can only be used if there is some degree of certainty of past wrongdoing. The person deserves to suffer because he committed an offense.

A **utilitarian** would argue that punishing past wrongs is not sufficient for the moral acceptability of inflicting harm; it should require good consequences for it to be morally acceptable.

Lawrence Hinman describes two types of **justification** for punishment:
1. Backward-looking, i.e., retribution
2. Forward-looking, i.e., deterrence, rehabilitation, reconciliation

The core concept of **retributivism** is that the offender should suffer at least as much as the victim did; *lex talionis*, or "an eye for an eye." Opponents argue that this is just revenge by another name. Hinman answers that retribution is more about resetting the moral balance, balancing the scales of justice, protecting the rights of victims, and about changing the offenders. Some retributivists contend that victims have a right to see their perpetrators suffer their punishment. Critics of retributivism ask if punishment is really justified. They state that this can lead to punishments that are cruel and that have no morally good effects.

Many who propose a forward-looking view contend that punishment has a deterrent effect on criminals and deters them from committing the same crime, as well as deterring others from committing that crime. Most research however, does not support this premise. Some object that rehabilitation would be too costly, and may conflict with the demands of retribution.

Many theorists worry that if we concentrate too much on punishment, this takes away from solving the social conditions, such as poverty, that give rise to crime. Perhaps drunk drivers brought to an accident scene might be more effectively rehabilitated. In the United States, we have a disproportionately large percentage of people in prison. Avoiding prison, which might be seen as a school for criminals, might be a better option.

Death Penalty

The Supreme Court decided that the death penalty would not be permitted for minors or crimes committed while a minor. In **Kennedy v. Louisiana (2008)**, Louisiana law was overturned to permit capital punishment for rape of a child. Two questions emerge:
1. Is death too severe a penalty to impose for any crime?

2. Is capital punishment compatible with our values about human dignity and decency?

In our society, murder is a crime for which the death penalty is often deemed appropriate. Not only has this person caused the death of another, but has undermined the fabric of a moral community.

Both opponents and defenders of capital punishment appeal to the **sanctity of life**. Opponents say life is sacred and no one should take it. Defenders, on the other hand, say that the way to honor the sanctity of life is to execute criminals who have taken someone's life.

War and Peace

War can be defined as an actual, intentional, and widespread armed conflict between political communities, motivated by significant disagreement over governance. War is a violent way to determine who gets to say what happens in a given territory, such as who gets wealth and resources, whose ideals prevail, how much tax is levied, etc. War is the last means for deciding these issues if an attempt at a peaceful process can't be agreed upon.

There are three main schools of thought on the ethics of war and peace: Just War Theory, Realism, and Pacifism.

Just War Theory is a synthesis of classical Greco-Roman, as well as Christian values. There are three parts to just war theory:

1. **Jus ad bellum**: for any war to be justified, a political community, or state, must fulfill all six of the following requirements:
    a) **Just cause**, e.g., self-defense from external attack, the protection of innocents from brutal, aggressive regimes, and punishment for sever wrongs that have not been corrected.
    b) **Right intention**, i.e., a state must intend to engage in war only for the sake of its just cause. The motivation behind resorting to war must be morally appropriate.
    c) **Proper authority and public declaration**, i.e., a state may only go to war if the decision has been made by the appropriate authorities, usually specified in that country's constitution.

Ethics: Theory and Practice

    d) **Last resort**, i.e., all other plausible and peaceful alternatives must have been exhausted to resolve the conflicts in question.

    e) **Probability of success**, i.e., if a positive impact on the situation cannot be anticipated, then war cannot be resorted to.

    f) **Proportionality**, i.e., before the war is started, a state must weigh the universal goods expected to result from it, against the universal evils, such as casualties.

(**Note**: The first three rules are *deontological* requirements, whereas the last three are *consequentialist*.)

2. **Jus in bello**: refers to the justice in war, to right conduct during battle. External, or traditional, *jus in bello*, refers to the rules regarding the enemy and its armed forces. The rules are:

    a) **Obey all international laws on weapons prohibition**, e.g., regarding chemical and biological weapons.

    b) **Discrimination and Non-Combatant Immunity**, i.e., a soldier must discriminate between those who are engaged in harm, and the civilian population that is morally immune from attack.

    c) **Proportionality**, i.e., the force used must be proportional to the end the soldiers seek.

    d) **Benevolent quarantine for prisoners of war (POWs),** i.e., once enemies surrender and become captives, they are no longer threats, so it is wrong to subject them to death, starvation, torture, medical experimentation, etc. There is still much controversy on the detainment and aggressive questioning of terrorist suspects.

    e) **No Means Mala in Se**, i.e., soldiers cannot use means that are evil in themselves, such as mass rape campaigns or genocide.

    f) **No Reprisals,** i.e., when Country A violates *jus in bello* in war with Country B, because these only serve to escalate death and make the destruction of war more indiscriminate.

(**Note**: Internal *jus in bello* involves the rules a state must follow regarding its own people as it battles against an enemy. These basically mean that human

rights are still respected as best they can during the crisis.)
3. **Jus post bellum**: refers to justice during the last stage of a war. The following principles must be considered:
    a) **Proportionality and Publicity**, i.e., a peace settlement needs to be measured and reasonable.
    b) **Rights Vindication**, i.e., the peace settlement should assure those rights whose violation prompted the justified war.
    c) **Discrimination**, i.e., distinction must be made between the leaders, combatants, and civilians of the defeated country.
    d) **Punishments #1**, i.e., if the country losing the war aggressively violated rights, then punishment must be appropriate. The leaders should face fair and public international trials for war crimes.
    e) **Punishment #2,** i.e., soldiers from all sides must be held accountable to investigation and possible trial.
    f) **Compensation**, i.e., a post-war poll tax on civilians is generally not allowed, and resources need to be adequate so that the defeated country can begin its own rebuilding.
    g) **Rehabilitation**, i.e., demilitarization and disarmament, police and judicial re- training, human rights education, etc.

(**Note**: Basically, there needs to be an ethical exit strategy from war.)

Realism

Realists believe that moral concepts should not be used as descriptions of, or prescriptions for, state behavior on an international level. Emphasis is on power and security issues, the need for a state to focus on it self-interest, and, most importantly, they view the international arena as a kind of anarchy, in which the will to power is priority. Once in a war, realists contend that a state must do whatever it can to win. (*All's fair in love and war.*)

1. **Descriptive realism** claims that states, as a matter of fact, either do not or cannot behave morally. Morality is a luxury states cannot afford.
2. **Prescriptive realism** claims that a state ought to behave amorally in the international arena. (*Nice guys finish last.*)
3.

Pacifism

A pacifist rejects war in favor of peace. War for the pacifist is always wrong;

there is no moral justification to resort to war. It is not violence that a pacifist necessarily objects to; it is the specific kind and degree of violence that war involves. A pacifist objects to killing, and especially the mass killing that is always part of a war.

Opponents of pacifism argue that the pacifist refuses to take part in defending himself and his country, but gathers all the benefits without sharing in the burdens.

Terrorism

Thomas Hobbes makes three points relevant to this issue:

1. He insists that **fear** is definitely a bad thing. To live in constant fear--not just occasional anxiety, but to have an unrelenting fear of violent death--is worse than anything. Fear controls and reduces a person. To live in continual fear is to have no life at all.
2. Fear is hardly compatible with **social life**. People who are afraid tend to stay alone with their fears and trust no one.
3. A condition of unrelenting fear can only be kept at bay in a **stable political society**.

Terrorism capitalizes on these points. Terrorists strike violence against civilians and noncombatants precisely to inflict fear or terror, with the aim of destabilizing the existing social order. This fear may provoke a lack of confidence in the government, depress the economy, and/or distort the political process.

Biomedical Ethics: Cloning to Produce Children

We will likely be reading about the controversial debate over human cloning for decades to come. This issue brings up countless moral, legal, and ethical questions. The first and most essential question is how human cloning would challenge the basic nature of human reproduction and the meaning of having children. Proponents have emphasized many possible uses of this technology, were it perfected:

1. Providing an infertile couple with a biologically related child
2. Allowing reproduction for same-sex couples or single individuals
3. Avoiding the risk of genetic diseases
4. Being able to have a genetically identical source of organs
5. Cloning individuals with great genius, talent or athletic ability

6. Replacing a loved spouse or child who has died

Arguments in Favor

Arguments for these suggested purposes for cloning-to-produce-children generally fall into three categories: human freedom, existence, and well-being.

1. **Human freedom**: The argument is not so much a support for cloning, but for the right to practice it. Because individuals define the good life and right and wrong differently, society is bound to protect individual freedom to choose, as long as their choices do not compromise the rights of others. But the right to reproduce cannot be ethically exercised without considering the child. Another argument proposes that human existence, by its very nature, is open-ended, indeterminate and unpredictable. New technologies are always evolving.

2. **The goodness of existence**: The appeal here again, is not so much an argument for cloning, as it is an argument against those who oppose cloning. They want to protect the cloned child-to-be against the risks and obvious unusual beginnings as a clone. Existence, in and of itself, is the first interest, and without cloning the child would not exist.

3. **The goodness of well-being:** This argument states that cloning would contribute to human goods deeply valued by society, e.g., the health of newborns, possibilities for the infertile couple, and the possibility of having a biologically related child. In situations such as these, cloning would relieve personal suffering, or prevent it in the future.

Arguments Against

Arguments against cloning-to-produce-children fall into two general categories:

1. **Problems of safety:** Cloning-to-produce-children is still not a safe procedure. There are safety concerns related to the potential dangers to the cloned child, to the egg donor, and to the woman who would carry the cloned child to birth. Because of these significant risks, those against cloning agree that this would constitute unethical experimentation on human subjects and is, therefore, impermissible. There should be guaranteed safety of the cloning procedure and the health of the participants. We can look at

the long-standing practice of regulating experiments on human subjects, such as the **Nuremberg Code** of 1947, the **Helsinki Declaration** of 1964, and more recently, the **Belmont Report** of 1978. It is our society's values that say that human beings cannot be treated as experimental guinea pigs for scientific research.

2. **Problems of exploitation of women:** Women would be called upon to donate eggs that would be required in extremely large numbers. This would involve hormonal treatments to produce super ovulation. Financial incentives might mean that poor women would place themselves at risk in this way.

The **ethical implications** of cloning-to-produce-children directly stem from the challenge this presents to the nature of human procreation and child rearing. Some of the compelling issues are:

1. Problems of identity and individuality
2. Concerns regarding manufacture, leading to genetic manipulation and genetic control
3. Prospect of a new eugenic, i.e., genetic enhancement
4. Troubled family relations
5. Effects on society, e.g., the hazards and costs of cloning

Environmental Ethics

Environmental ethics extends to the traditional boundaries of ethics to include the non-human world. When studying environmental ethics, the most fundamental question is, "What obligations do we have concerning the natural environment?" If the answer is that we, as human beings, will die if we do not constrain our actions toward nature, then that ethic is considered to be anthropocentric. Determining whether our environmental obligations are founded on anthropocentric on non-anthropocentric reasoning will lead to different conclusions of what those obligations are. Anthropocentrism (ethical humanism), biocentrism (eco-centrism), and land ethics (eco-holism) are discussed in detail in Chapter 9.

Practical applications of environmental ethics are evident in such arenas a business, government, and lifestyle choices. Many businesses deal with issues such as industrial waste disposal, natural resource usage, packaging design, transportation choices, and energy consumption. The federal government is responsible for the national park system, the Environmental Protection Agency (EPA), and for creating legislation that regulates impacts on air and water, among other natural resources. Local governments deal with recycling and waste disposal issues, sewer and water authorities, and hunting and fishing regulations. Lifestyle choices based on environmental ethics can include vegetarianism or veganism, organic farming, gardening, and shopping, recycling and composting, re-purposing and buying second-hand.

Ethics: Theory and Practice

Answers for Chapter Review Questions

Chapter 1:   1) b,   2) c,   3) a,   4) a,   5) d

Chapter 2:   1) c,   2) e,   3) b,   4) a,   5) d

Chapter 3:   1) c,   2) d,   3) c,   4) c,   5) a

Chapter 4:   1) d,   2) b,   3) d,   4) b,   5) b

Chapter 5:   1) c,   2) a,   3) b,   4) a,   5) c

Chapter 6:   1) b,   2) a,   3) d,   4) a,   5) b

Chapter 7:   1) c,   2) b,   3) b,   4) b,   5) a

Chapter 8:   1) c,   2) b,   3) a,   4) b,   5) a,   6) c

Chapter 9:   1) a,   2) d,   3) b,   4) d,   5) c

Chapter 10: 1) d,   2) c,   3) d,   4) a,   5) d

Chapter 11: 1) b,   2) d,   3) d,   4) a,   5) b

Ethics: Theory and Practice

PRACTICE EXAM

Directions: Each of the 130 questions or incomplete statements below is followed by four suggested answers or completions. Select the one that is best in each case.

1. Which of the following best describes the midway point between excess and deficiency?
    A. Surplus balance
    B. Virtuous point
    C. Excess/deficiency line
    D. Moral virtue

2. Which of the following statements best describes ethics?
    A. A branch of philosophy that uses reason to support positions
    B. It is similar to the Golden Rule
    C. A cross-generational set of beliefs about right and wrong
    D. Behavior that is agreed upon to be moral by the majority

3. What is Euthyphro?
    A. The relationship of humans and gods
    B. The comparison of gods to humans
    C. The nature of goodness
    D. The practice of wisdom

4. Which of the following best describes an ethical theory?
    A. It provides norms for judging acts to be right or wrong and attempts to give a justification for these norms
    B. It deals with ideas about right and wrong
    C. It provides norms for judging acts to be right or wrong while withholding justification for the norms
    D. It cannot be used as sole justification of an act

5. What best describes meta-ethics?
    A. The study of thinking about ethics
    B. The meanings of ethical language
    C. Historical literature about ethics
    D. The study of the practicality of ethical decisions

Ethics: Theory and Practice

6. Which of the following is NOT a reason for supporting ethical relativism?
    A. Uncertainty about morals
    B. Differences in moral views
    C. Social cohesion
    D. Situational differences

7. Which of the following in NOT a reason given for developing our natural moral reasoning skills?
    A. The diversity of the community necessitates values built of reason
    B. As we develop our skills, we will be able to win more ethical arguments
    C. People of all walks of life should be able to have healthy conversations with one another
    D. We should have the capacity to know what's right and wrong

8. This writer was considered to be one of the most intelligent men of his time. He is generally held to be one of the most profound and effective spokesmen for the utilitarian view. He was also a strong supporter of personal liberty while strongly criticizing society for its treatment of women. His name was:
    A. Immanuel Kant
    B. John Stuart Mill
    C. James Stewart
    D. Aristotle

9. What are the principles of morality, according to Hume?
    A. They are derived from moral sentiments, not reason
    B. They are derived from how a person feels in the moment
    C. They are derived from early experiences
    D. They are derived from cross-generational values

10. Which of the following is NOT important to making a good argument?
    A. How much of the argument is based on logic
    B. How much of the argument is based on personal experience
    C. The structure of the argument itself
    D. The argument leads to the right conclusion

Ethics: Theory and Practice

11. Which of the following best describes The Ring of Gyges?
    A. A ring that represents pure morality
    B. A ring that can make one wiser
    C. A ring that can make the wearer invisible
    D. A geological formation resembling a ring

12. Which of the following terms best describes what happens when a person's liberty may be restricted to prevent them from doing harmful things to themselves?
    A. Legal paternalism
    B. Power of attorney
    C. The defense principle
    D. Natural danger theory

13. What is another name for a good argument?
    A. A solid argument
    B. A sound argument
    C. A just argument
    D. A winning argument

14. What are the two basic types of virtue, according to Aristotle?
    A. Moral and practical
    B. Intellectual and moral
    C. Practical and intellectual
    D. Theoretical and moral

15. What is a guiding principle of ethical relativism?
    A. All actions are equally moral
    B. No one can really know right and wrong
    C. There is no objective right and wrong
    D. Everyone should have the same morals

16. Which of the following people was NOT one of the founders of utilitarianism?
    A. Rene Descartes
    B. James Mill
    C. John Stuart Mill
    D. Jeremy Bentham

Ethics: Theory and Practice

17. What does Glaucon want to demonstrate by giving rings to two people?
    A. Relativism
    B. That people are as wise as the gods
    C. That even "good" people will do evil if they can act without consequence
    D. That people with the most power form the strongest bonds

18. What are hypothetical imperatives?
    A. Complicated manners of behaving
    B. Things that must be done no matter what
    C. Suggestions that we should use what works to arrive at a goal
    D. Actions all people should take to arrive at the same goal

19. According to the utilitarianism viewpoint, which of the following is useful for evaluating the morality of an action?
    A. The result
    B. The type of action
    C. Accomplishing the goal
    D. The behavior of the person(s) involved

20. Which of the following statements expresses the correlativity thesis regarding rights?
    A. Rights imply entitled behaviors
    B. Rights are the same across the globe
    C. Rights all depend on the situation
    D. Rights entail obligations and vice versa

21. How would a utilitarian regard abortion?
    A. "Wrong" because it shouldn't be a choice
    B. They would perform a cost-benefit analysis
    C. "Right" because it appears to render an outcome that benefits a lot of people
    D. Immoral because it destroys life

22. Moral "oughts" are all of the following EXCEPT_____:
    A. The belief in equality
    B. They are supported by laws

C. The similarity of people
D. A necessity

23. How does rule utilitarianism ask that we consider the consequences of each of our actions?
    A. On a specific smaller scale
    B. According to a set of already defined rules
    C. On a sporadic basis
    D. As a general practice

24. What does the first categorical imperative state?
    A. To engage in acts that result in justice
    B. To act on the maxim that you can will, as a universal law
    C. To do no harm to others
    D. To put things into perspective by being organized in cognitions

25. Natural law is the most similar to _____.
    A. Moral law
    B. Ethical law
    C. Practicality law
    D. Theoretical law

26. Which of the following is an intrinsic good, according to utilitarianism?
    A. Social justice
    B. Pleasure
    C. Autonomy
    D. Power

27. Which of the following is NOT necessary to act morally, according to utilitarianism?
    A. To consider all variables involved
    B. To regard everyone as equals
    C. To consider producing the greatest results for the greatest amount of people
    D. To act as the majority desires

28. Which of the following statements is false about natural rights?
    A. They are discovered through reason
    B. They are based upon human nature

C. They are the foundation of most religious writings

D. They are essential for our everyday functioning as people

29. What is natural law?

   A. Hypothetical

   B. Teleological

   C. Metaphorical

   D. Metaphysical

30. What has the highest intrinsic value, according to Immanuel Kant?

   A. People

   B. Love

   C. Power

   D. Justice

31. What do negative rights imply?

   A. That other should have conventional rights

   B. That others do not have natural rights

   C. That everyone has natural rights

   D. That others should refrain from interfering with those rights

32. According to Kant, the highest moral activity happens as a result of _____.

   A. Putting the needs of others before our own

   B. Putting the rights of others before our own

   C. Acting out of a will to do the right thing

   D. Acting based on past experience

33. What is the good, according to Aristotle?

   A. That which brings about the most happiness

   B. The best option, considering the circumstances

   C. That which results in the most power

   D. The end to which all things aim

34. What do virtue ethics help us determine?

   A. How we ought to be

   B. The morality of an action

   C. Cross-generational morals

   D. How others should behave

Ethics: Theory and Practice

35. Which of the following is used by the American Medical Association to define "dead"?
    A. When the spirit leaves the body
    B. Whole brain death has occurred
    C. Heart has stopped beating
    D. When the person has lost all mental functioning

36. Man's sense of virtue is thought to emphasize _____.
    A. Rights over responsibility
    B. Consequences before actions
    C. Justice over relationship
    D. Individualism over collectivism

37. Which of the following is true, according to W.D. Ross?
    A. Loyalty is more important than honesty
    B. The relationship between honesty and loyalty is conditional
    C. Loyalty and honesty are unrelated constructs
    D. Honesty is more important than loyalty

38. What is the unique element of human beings, according to Aristotle?
    A. The development of pure relationships
    B. The "morality effect"
    C. The "immortal soul"
    D. The "rational element"

39. Which of the following best describes Kant's second form of the categorical imperative?
    A. The "Golden Rule"
    B. Think about all the consequences before acting
    C. Regard yourself as number one
    D. Don't use people unless it is in their best interest

40. What happens in an argument based on analogy?
    A. Both parties agree to disagree
    B. The argument becomes invalid
    C. One compares familiar examples with the issue being disputed
    D. The argument becomes about assumptions

Ethics: Theory and Practice

41. Harry tries to make his wife happy by giving her freshly cut roses. His wife is an environmentalist who strongly opposes the destruction of nature and becomes sad when she receives the flowers. According to _____, _____.
    A. Consequentialists, the giving of cut flowers is wrong
    B. The deontological theory, the giving of cut flowers is wrong
    C. Teleological theory, the giving of cut flowers is wrong
    D. A and C are correct

42. Which of the following is closely related to Roe v. Wade?
    A. Virtue ethics
    B. Categorical imperative
    C. Egoism
    D. Utilitarianism

43. Where Kant took morality to be a given, to be clarified, justified but not questioned, who _____ viewed morality not as a given, but as a strictly human invention that was tyrannical and destructive?
    A. Friedrich Nietzsche
    B. Aristotle
    C. John Stuart Mill
    D. Jeremy Bentham

44. _____ euthanasia is the same as mercy killing.
    A. Active involuntary
    B. Passive involuntary
    C. Inactive voluntary
    D. Active voluntary

45. Which of the following best describes the belief that gay and lesbian individuals should live openly in same-sex relationships, because doing so invites homophobic people to become more open and inclusive?
    A. Utilitarianism
    B. Kantian reasoning
    C. Egalitarianism

Ethics: Theory and Practice

    D. Egoism

46. What is true about "the veil of ignorance?"
    A. Its goals is to eliminate personal biases
    B. It serves to define choices performed in the "original location"
    C. It is part of Rawls's theory of justice
    D. All of the above

47. Which of the following would describe the notion that sex is only acceptable between consenting adults?
    A. Sexual morality
    B. Virtue ethics
    C. Kantian ethics
    D. Utilitarianism

48. Why should the possessor of the ring still act morally, according to Plato's *The Ring of Gyges* story?
    A. Because we should always act altruistically
    B. Because self-control is a virtue
    C. Because simply appearing moral means we are moral
    D. Because harmony should always be the top priority

49. Which of the following is an example of extraordinary intervention?
    A. Transference
    B. Transfusion
    C. Transmission
    D. Transplant

50. Which of the following is NOT listed among the liberty-limiting principles?
    A. The social harm principle
    B. The offense principle
    C. The minor protection principle
    D. The defense principle

51. What is the best example of the categorical imperative?
    A. If everyone practiced homosexual sex, there would be no children
    B. Homosexual sex is not natural
    C. We were not designed to have sex with same-sex partners

D. Homophobia is destructive for offspring

52. People who argue that abortions lead to a lack of adoptable babies are basing their argument on:
    A. Virtue ethics
    B. Egoism
    C. Utilitarianism
    D. The offense principle

53. With regards to pornography, which of the following is true about the harm principle?
    A. That people who are into pornography always do harm
    B. That people who view pornography make everyday living dangerous
    C. That people who view pornography rarely do harm to others
    D. That people act out pornographic impressions in real life

54. To suggest that abortion may be less immoral in Kenya than in Germany is based on which of the following?
    A. Relativism
    B. Conventional law
    C. Categorical imperative
    D. Egoism

55. Which of the following is the primary focus of virtue ethics?
    A. Happiness
    B. Power
    C. Character
    D. Compassion

56. Which of the following best describes the notion that homosexuality is permissible as long as it is agreed upon by the participants?
    A. The ideas of natural law
    B. Conventional law
    C. Kantian reasoning
    D. Altruism

57. Who referred to what he called the "original position" as an indicator of equality?
    A. John Stuart Mill

B. John Rawls
C. Immanuel Kant
D. Aristotle

58. Affirmative action plans must be adopted by:
A. All companies that have more than 50 employees and receive $50,000 or more in federal money
B. All companies with over 100 full-time employees
C. All companies with over 1000 employees
D. All companies that receive any amount of federal money

59. What is choosing the mean likely to result in, according to Aristotle?
A. Happiness
B. Power
C. Virtue
D. Justice

60. Which of the following is an example of the natural law position?
A. Denying one's sexual identity can lead to major consequences
B. Human nature should be considered when making choices about sex
C. Everyone should consider the needs of others no matter what
D. Things will happen naturally if we allow them to

61. What is the principle of justice?
A. Like cases are to be treated alike
B. People should all live altruistically
C. Rules should be followed no matter the situation
D. We should respect each other's morals

62. What is the term used to describe the rights that are had by all people of based on the virtue of common humanity?
A. Extrinsic
B. Positive
C. Intrinsic
D. Relativistic

63. Legal paternalism refers to preventing people who view

pornography from doing harm to _____.
   A. Themselves
   B. The justice system
   C. Society as a whole
   D. Children

64. According to _____, we can determine basic moral principles by appealing to God's will.
   A. Egoism
   B. Religious relativism
   C. Utilitarianism
   D. Divine command theory

65. Which of the following is an example of whether or not affirmative action does more harm than good?
   A. Violation of natural law
   B. Altruism theory
   C. The consequentialist consideration
   D. Utilitarianism

66. Which of the following moral theories is one that is both axiological and consequential?
   A. Teleological
   B. Non-teleological
   C. Ontological
   D. Deontological

67. Which of the following would appeal to those who argue that animals have rights?
   A. Social relativism
   B. Utilitarianism
   C. Natural law
   D. Natural conservatism

68. What is moral virtue, according to Aristotle?
   A. Using one's character to gain popularity
   B. A disposition to choose the mean
   C. Acting ethically in most situations
   D. Obeying all laws of society

Ethics: Theory and Practice

69. When thinking about the anthropocentric perspective, the idea that we should curtail human activities to preserve a non-human species is generally anchored in which of the following theories?
    A. Social relativism
    B. Natural conservatism
    C. Natural selection
    D. Utilitarianism

70. Which type of reasoning would appeal to animal experimentation?
    A. Egoism
    B. Utilitarian
    C. Natural law
    D. Nature's law

71. Which of the following is related to the idea that allowing people to earn as much money as they can because doing so gives them incentive to be maximally productive?
    A. Categorical imperative
    B. Natural law
    C. Social relativism
    D. Utilitarianism

72. Who is the most notable proponent of rational egoism?
    A. Immanuel Kant
    B. Ayn Rand
    C. John Stuart Mill
    D. Aristotle

73. Which of the following does John Rawls say is a common meaning of the term "justice"?
    A. Receiving what one deserves
    B. Not inappropriately showing preferences
    C. Receiving what one deserves
    D. All of the above

74. Those that oppose affirmative action claim that because it is based on race, gender, or ethnicity, it is not consistent with _____ A. Free speech
    B. Altruism

C. Symbolic expression
D. Justice

75. What kind of reasoning would best describe the suggestion that capital punishment is a different moral question for nomadic peoples living in tents or other temporary shelters than for societies with maximum security prisons is what kind of reasoning?
   A. Relativism
   B. Natural law
   C. Kantian
   D. Global differentiation

76. The difference between teleological and deontological is _____.
   A. Deontological is moral and teleological is immoral
   B. Teleological focuses on intention and deontological focuses on motive
   C. Deontological is focused on intention and teleological is focused on consequence
   D. Teleological is moral and deontological is immoral

77. How does Kant define perfect duties?
   A. Obligations that no one person has a right to have performed for his/her benefit
   B. Obligations that bring out the best in people
   C. Obligations in which a person has a right to have that obligation performed
   D. Obligations that are bound by law

78. How do emotivists view moral arguments?
   A. As expressions of deep-seeded trauma
   B. As expressions of attitudes
   C. As expressions of convention
   D. As expressions of social justice

79. What would Mill argue if a person had to lie in order to save somebody's life?
   A. Morality cannot provide a clear answer in this situation
   B. S/he should do what makes them feel good

C. S/he should not lie because lying is always wrong
D. S/he should lie, because the utility of saving a life outweighs the claims of justice

80. On what form of moral reasoning does egocentrism rely?
    A. Social justice
    B. Natural law
    C. Utilitarianism
    D. Social relativism

81. Which type of reasoning was utilized by William Baxter?
    A. Anthropocentric
    B. Egocentric
    C. Relativism
    D. Anthropological

For questions 82-86, consider the following case study:

Lisa is 5 months pregnant and was at risk for losing the fetus several times. Doctors managed to save the pregnancy by hospitalizing her since the pregnancy began (i.e., she has been in the hospital for five months). Unfortunately, she developed personal health complications directly related to the pregnancy. Her doctors informed her that she is at great risk for stroke and death if she continues with the pregnancy. She is also told that the fetus is significantly underdeveloped and most likely would not survive outside the womb. Lisa loves being pregnant and enjoys having children around her to nurture. She feels motherhood is her one true calling and she naturally does it well. Her husband, Joe, supports her decisions. Lisa's father, a devout Catholic, is strongly against abortion. Lisa's mother has been helping Joe take care of two young children, both at home and under eight years of age. Lisa's mother has told Lisa several times that it is exhausting for her and Joe to take care of the two children.

82. Who holds utilitarian views?
    A. Lisa's mother
    B. Lisa's father
    C. Lisa's physician
    D. Joe

83. What can be assumed about Lisa's views?
    A. They are based on ethics of care
    B. They are based on the principles of the divine command theory
    C. They are egocentric
    D. Both A and B

84. Whose behavior is altruistic?
    A. Lisa's father's behavior
    B. Lisa's physician's behavior
    C. Lisa's mother's behavior
    D. All of the above

85. Who does not have egotistical views?
    A. Lisa's mother
    B. Joe
    C. Lisa
    D. None of the above

86. Who has views that are most like the divine command theory?
    A. Joe
    B. Lisa's physician
    C. Lisa's mother
    D. Lisa's father

87. What must we examine during philosophical analysis?
    A. Reasons for our moral beliefs
    B. Processes that lead to decision making
    C. Moral beliefs behind our justifications
    D. Reasons for our actions

For questions 88-93, consider the following scenario:

Six siblings own some untouched woodland property that lies adjacent to a public park. The land loaded with fossil fuels. Recently, the availability of fossil fuels and lumber has decreased, halting the building of homes, schools, churches, and other wooden structures throughout the country. In addition, all products related to fossil fuels have become scarce. Lastly, the price of both lumber and fossil fuels has made them unattainable for the vast majority of individuals. Read the following dialogue and answer the questions afterward.

Sibling A: I think we should leave the land exactly as it is. I don't want to remove even a single tree. The system should remain intact and not be impacted in any unnatural way.

Sibling B: We ought to take out just a few trees, so the remaining trees can fill in and not be choked out. We can then take those few trees and sell them. Doing this, we can minimize impact while simultaneously providing some much needed lumber for others…and money for us!

Sibling C: Wait a minute "B!" I agree with "A." The value in our land lies in its beauty! Listen to it, let others look and listen. They will experience something they can't possibly experience anywhere else. Let's not touch it.

Sibling D: Enough of this babble! Don't you three realize that without homes and fuel people will freeze and die? Even one death is too many. This land is here for our use. Owning it is only worth it if we use it to help our fellow man. I vote we cut some trees and mine some fossil fuels. Heck, making money isn't important here…but helping others is. Helping others would be the highest good that could come from our land.

Sibling E: I agree with "D." We should do what benefits the most people.

Sibling F: Nature is good, right, and well-balanced. Any intrusion we make into the land must be justified.

88. Which of the following is most like Sibling C's view?
    A. Ralph Waldo Emerson
    B. Henry David Thoreau
    C. Ecocentrism
    D. All of the above

89. Sibling A's view is most like which of the following?
    A. Aldo Leopold
    B. Immanuel Kant

C. John Stuart Mill
D. Aristotle

90. Which of the following most closely matches Sibling D's viewpoint?
   A. Instrumental
   B. Nicomachean ethics
   C. Anthropocentrism
   D. All of the above

91. Sibling E's view is most like:
   A. Henry David Thoreau
   B. John Stuart Mill
   C. Kantian ethics
   D. None of the above

92. Sibling B's view is most like:
   A. Aristotle
   B. A cost-benefit analysis
   C. Deep ecology
   D. John Rawls

93. Sibling F's view is most like which of the following?
   A. Anthropocentrism
   B. Egocentrism
   C. Deep ecology
   D. Kantian ethics

94. The claim that "sometimes euthanasia is permissible" belongs to which of the following?
   A. Applied ethics
   B. Descriptive ethics
   C. None of the above
   D. Both A and B

95. What is the term used to describe when an ethical judgment is based upon empirical or experiential information?
   A. Proven
   B. A normative judgment
   C. A well-known fact

Ethics: Theory and Practice

    D. A descriptive judgment

96. How is virtue learned?
    A. By role modeling
    B. By successful mentoring
    C. By habit
    D. By learning lessons from our past mistakes

97. Why is the question "why be moral?" more met ethical than ethical?
    A. Because it gives non-moral reasons for why someone should be moral
    B. Because it deals more with how people make decisions
    C. Because it deals with what makes actions moral or immoral, right or wrong
    D. Because it concerns everyone on a global scale

98. What is the tem used to describe if an ethical judgment is based upon beliefs in general about what is good or right?
    A. Categorical imperative
    B. A longstanding social belief
    C. Normative judgment
    D. Causative judgment

99. What is the study of the meaning of ethical language?
    A. Metacommunication
    B. Philosophy
    C. Communicative morals
    D. Meta-ethics

100. Moral realism refers to morality that is _____.
    A. Just and true
    B. Real and tangible
    C. Independent of what is witnessed
    D. Proven through observation

101. John Rawls was primarily interested in what type of questions?
    A. Distributive justice
    B. Individual rights
    C. Meta-ethical

D. Social relativism

102. Which of the following types of argument is a case for affirmative action based on justice?
   A. Offense principle
   B. Non-consequentialist
   C. Consequentialist
   D. Contraction

103. Speciesism is _____.
   A. A prejudice in favor of one's own species over another
   B. Equality of all species
   C. Power of one species over another
   D. None of the above

104. How are justice and virtue different?
   A. Justice deals with our relations to others, while virtue is a state of being
   B. Justice is global while virtue is local
   C. Justice is a manmade construct, while virtue is more natural
   D. They are the same thing

105. In which case did the Illinois Supreme Court rule that the swastika is a symbolic expression?
   A. Cohen v. California (1968)
   B. National Socialist Party of America v. Village of Skokie (1977
   C. Chaplinsky v. New Hampshire (1942)
   D. American Booksellers v. Hudnut (1985)

106. What two types of freedom were defined by Simone de Beauvoir?
   A. Free will and symbolic freedom
   B. Authentic freedom and symbolic freedom
   C. Virtuous freedom and free will
   D. Creative freedom and free will

107. Which argument implies that failure of affirmative action to meet the conditions of justice might be outweighed by the important social good it produces?
   A. Social justice
   B. Social inequality

C. Social utility
D. Reverse discrimination

108. It is unjust to treat people differently in ways that deny some of them significant social benefits unless we can show that there is a difference between them that is relevant to the differential treatment. This statement is a definition of which of the following?
　A. Natural law
　B. Social justice
　C. The defense principle
　D. The principle of equality

109. What did Helen Longino define as verbal or pictorial explicit representations of sexual behavior that have, as a distinguishing characteristic, the degrading and demeaning portrayal of the role and status of the human female as a mere sexual object to be exploited and manipulated sexually?
　A. Pornography
　B. Sexual material
　C. Sexually-charged material
　D. Sexual discrimination

110. To appeal to the value of personal autonomy in euthanasia decisions is to appeal to what kind of reason/norm?
　A. Consequentialist
　B. Ontological
　C. Non-consequentialist
　D. Teleological

111. With what is the principle of double effect concerned?
　A. Doubling the effects of the actions on outcomes
　B. Foreseeing an end versus intending it
　C. Both of the above
　D. Neither of the above

112. John Stuart Mill wrote _____.
　A. *On Liberty*
　B. *The Ethics of Ambiguity*
　C. *Genealogy of Morals*
　D. *The Republic*

Ethics: Theory and Practice

113. What does the term "extraordinary measures" apply to?
    A. Treatments that are life-changing
    B. Treatments that are underground and illegal
    C. Treatments with no reasonable hope of benefit
    D. Treatments that are very costly

114. Pro-choice activists might argue that abortion is warranted if, in an individual case, the benefits outweigh any costs or negative effects to the intended. This could be labeled as _____?
    A. Deontological
    B. Utilitarian
    C. Ontological
    D. Teleological

115. What does G.E. Moore state in his 1903 book, *Principia Ethica,* that is an alleged mistake in ethics that involves defining "good" in naturalistic terms?
    A. Virtuous realism
    B. Social unawareness
    C. Slippery slope
    D. Naturalistic fallacy

116. John Stuart Mill was a _____.
    A. Social constructivist
    B. Utilitarian
    C. Deontologist
    D. Egoist

117. Simone de Beauvoir describes the widespread attitude of bad faith and attributes it to the person she identifies as what?
    A. Powerful individual
    B. Serious individual
    C. Inauthentic individual
    D. Authentic individual

118. Which of the following is NOT a prima facie duty, according to W.D. Ross?
    A. Duty of beneficence
    B. Duty of justice

C. Duty of religion
D. Duty of non-malfeasance

119. Nihilism is defined as _____.
    A. The belief in nothing
    B. The belief that one is better than others
    C. The belief that values and morals are determined by God
    D. The belief that morals should benefit the greater good

120. Eudemonia refers to _____ in virtue ethics.
    A. Loss of faith in humanity
    B. Achievement and money
    C. Shame and guilt
    D. Human flourishing and success

121. Nietzsche claims that in order to remain free and gain our own perspective, we should not allow ourselves to be dominated by a particular will. This is an example of which of the following terms?
    A. Egocentrism
    B. Perspectivism
    C. Mental strength
    D. Altruism

122. What view holds that all moral statements are false?
    A. Cognitivist anti-realism
    B. Intuitionism
    C. Moral realism
    D. Nihilism

123. What has intrinsic value, according to anthropocentrism?
    A. All species and organisms
    B. Humans and chimpanzees
    C. Humans only
    D. All life forms with higher intelligence

124. What kind of justice is founded on the notion of merit?
    A. Social
    B. Retributive
    C. Distributive
    D. Procedural

125. The freedom to speak freely without censorship or limitation is referred to as _____.
   A. Freedom of expression
   B. Symbolic expression
   C. Unlimited communications
   D. Free speech

126. What kind of justice is concerned with making and implementing decisions according to fair processes because fair procedures are the best guarantee for fair outcomes?
   A. Distributive
   B. Universal
   C. Procedural
   D. Retributive

127. Which of the following is NOT an example of moral legalism?
   A. Divine command theory
   B. Utilitarianism
   C. Ethical egotism
   D. Nihilism

128. Who believed that the goal of distributive justice was to limit the influence of luck so that goods might be distributed in a way that is both equally fair and to everyone's advantage?
   A. John Rawls
   B. John Stuart Mill
   C. Aristotle
   D. John Rawls

129. What principle states that social and economic inequalities should be to the greatest benefit of the least advantaged members of society?
   A. Difference
   B. Distributive
   C. Retributive
   D. Procedural

130. According to which principle should our moral opinions be based on nothing more than feelings?
    A. Ethical universalism
    B. Subjectivism
    C. Non-relativism
    D. Emotive realism

Ethics: Theory and Practice

PRACTICE EXAM ANSWER KEY

1. D	2. A	3. C
4. A	5. B	6. C
7. B	8. B	9. A
10. D	11. C	12. A
13. B	14. B	15. C
16. A	17. C	18. C
19. A	20. D	21. C
22. B	23. D	24. B
25. A	26. B	27. D
28. C	29. B	30. A
31. D	32. C	33. D
34. A	35. B	36. C
37. B	38. D	39. D
40. C	41. D	42. D
43. A	44. A	45. B
46. D	47. C	48. B
49. D	50. C	51. A
52. C	53. D	54. A
55. C	56. A	57. B
58. A	59. C	60. B
61. A	62. B	63. A
64. D	65. C	66. A
67. C	68. B	69. D
70. B	71. D	72. B

Ethics: Theory and Practice

73. D	74. D	75. A
76. C	77. C	78. B
79. D	80. B	81. A
82. C	83. A	84. C
85. B	86. D	87. A
88. D	89. A	90. D
91. B	92. B	93. C
94. A	95. D	96. C
97. A	98. C	99. D
100. D	101. A	102. B
103. A	104. A	105. B
106. D	107. C	108. D
109. A	110. C	111. B
112. A	113. C	114. B
115. D	116. B	117. B
118. C	119. A	120. D
121. B	122. A	123. C
124. B	125. D	126. C
127. D	128. A	129. A
130. B		

www.ingramcontent.com/pod-product-compliance
Lightning Source LLC
Chambersburg PA
CBHW082124230426
43671CB00015B/2793